Let the healing begin!

Dick Greenwood

THE —— OBSERVER'S CHAIR

Special Gift Edition

To: _____

From: _____

— THE —
OBSERVER'S
CHAIR

The Miracle of Healing Self-Esteem

Dave Blanchard

CEO, *The Og Mandino Group*

OgPress

The Observer's Chair: The Miracle of Healing Self-Esteem
Dave Blanchard

Library of Congress Cataloging-in-Publication Data
The Observer's Chair / Dave Blanchard
Library of Congress Control Number: 2012920440

ISBN 978-1-60645-115-1

Published by

OgPress

www.ogmandino.com

Author's Special Limited Gift Edition Printing

PRINTED IN THE UNITED STATES OF AMERICA

This book is dedicated to my wife and sweetheart, Ramona, who have given me a safe place to begin the journey of healing my self-esteem.

I want to thank my father and angel mother, Tom and RaNae Blanchard, for their encouragement in writing this book. Each generation can only build on the foundation provided by the previous.

I want to thank my coaching clients, literally thousands of amazing individuals, for having the courage to engage in life and embrace these principles. Each has been an inspiration and a joy to serve.

I want to thank good friends who responded quickly and who provided sound advice and guidance—all in an effort to ensure that the words to follow are as powerful as we all want them to be. Bill Chalmers, Tobi Bishop, Barb Osier, Niki Preisley, Fran Platt, Karen Christoffersen, and Bill Ruesch.

TABLE OF CONTENTS

Prologue:
IT'S PERSONAL

Within me burns a flame, which has been passed from generations uncounted, and its heat is a constant irritation to my spirit to become better than I am, and I will. I will fan this flame of dissatisfaction and proclaim my uniqueness to the world.

— OG MANDINO

EVERY WEEK DAY MORNING and for four years running, and often on weekends, I arose at 4 a.m. and would write until 8 a.m. I was driven by one visual—a grown man weeping aloud, disillusioned, broke, broken, and angry because he was unable to magically manifest in tangible reality that which he had vividly visualized with great intention.

"I can see it so clearly. I can almost touch it. I can almost taste it," he exclaimed with a trembling voice. "Why can't *I* have it? What is wrong with me?" He then paused, lowered his head, and with resignation whispered, "Does God not love me?"

Over the years that followed, I assessed literally thousands of people actively seeking success who were silently and privately mumbling under their breath a similar toxic and self-deprecating dialogue.

An unmistakable pattern began to emerge in their Intentional Creation Assessments. The vast majority had vivid thoughts that were creating unrealistic expectations. Like dominos, every time life showed up differently than these expectations, they had thoughts that were fostering feelings of frustration, overwhelm, despair, and discouragement. These negative feelings in turn created thoughts that supported this self-deprecating dialogue—"What is wrong with me?"

This cascading sequence, which was becoming increasingly frequent, spurred other damaging thought processes. The most destructive were thoughts that drive comparison. By early 2009, these damaging thoughts were occurring with alarming rapidity.

I was able to serve my personal coaching clients who were initially stuck in these patterns by sharing the foundational principles, practices, and processes that govern the creation of our hopes and dreams. But what could I do to serve everyone else?

The answer was to write a book. In February 2012, we released, *Today I Begin a New Life*. This book outlined in great detail three of the Qualities of an Intentional Creator: The Art of Connection, Mental Creation, and Physical Creation.

A few weeks ago, while on a conference call with Joe Soto, our social media guru, and his amazing marketing team at One Social Media, the topic of healing self-esteem was raised. In passing, Joe asked if I would be willing to write a simple ten-page e-Book on the topic. He thought it would assist in their marketing efforts.

A lot of exciting things were discussed during that meeting, but I could only focus on one—the e-Book on healing self-esteem. This was the unspoken, underlying theme and natural outcome of applying the principles shared in the first book. However, in the last edit, at the final moment, the decision had been made to tackle the specifics of healing self-esteem at a later date in a second book.

While sitting there at my desk, listening to this conversation, I became acutely aware of just how much I regretted that decision. A short and substantive e-Book would be the perfect solution. Immediately after the call I scheduled an evening to accomplish the task.

What happened next was wholly unexpected. One night quickly turned into thirty and the initial ten-page request turned into a full second book. Driven by inspired ideas and impressions that ignited my passion, I often wrote through the night and with a deep sense of urgency. It was clear. There is a very real need for the words that follow.

Fellow Traveler

Ramona and I have known the dark night. We lost millions of dollars in 1988-89 during the collapse of the real estate market in Southern California. Financially, we found ourselves starting over at negative $1 million. It would take ten years to pay back that debt, all the while raising seven amazing children.

At times it was embarrassing and frightening. The journey required tenacity, persistence, and focused work. However and for me, the pain in this loss and the struggles required in repaying the debt and rebuilding our estate paled in comparison to my life-long struggle with a challenged self-esteem.

As a young boy, I found solace in the privacy of my room—I was safe there. For many years, I felt isolated, alone, a misfit, a stranger in a strange land. The world being what it is, the day came when I had to venture out—out there where I had been deeply wounded by two pedophiles.

My innocent parents had entrusted them with my well-being while dad attended college and mom worked. I was five when the living nightmare ended, but that was just the beginning of the journey.

The effort required just to leave my house and go to school was exhausting. When faced with the prospect of having to connect with someone, I wanted to run home and hide.

Friends were few. Then my first best friend accidently hung himself during the summer between second and third grade. I would hear the news from my mother while sitting on the grass in the southwest corner of our front yard. It would be five years before I would make another attempt at friendship.

Every three years we moved. This was necessary to advance my father's burgeoning career in the aerospace industry. Dad was a good man, a faithful husband and an excellent provider. Nevertheless, moving made it difficult to develop badly needed socialization skills. I was awkward, tongue-tied, self-conscious, and drowning in self-doubt. In short, I was uncomfortable in my own skin.

With time, the solace and safety only found in my childhood sanctuary was replaced with a quiet confidence that a person can rise above the past and heal their self-esteem. Though the details of our unique life experiences may differ, our innate desire to heal is so similar.

It's important to clearly state that I am a coach and not a therapist. When faced with healing self-esteem, some may need the skill of a good therapist to navigate potentially perilous waters in order to process painful life experiences. In this book, we find the principles, practices, and processes for those who are ready to move forward.

It is my desire to build a bridge to your heart so that my love—agape love—my heightened level of awareness on this tender topic—can enter your soul. When it does, it is my hope that you will want to share this new awareness with others.

Kevin Hall writes in his bestselling book, *Aspire:*

In old Hungary, along the Danube River between Budapest

*and Vienna, there was a village by the name of Kocs that pro-
duced the world's finest horse drawn vehicles...Originally
crafted for aristocracy, coaches carried important people
to their desired destinations in luxury...A 'coach' remains
something, or someone, who carries a valued person from
where they are to where they want to be.*

A coach carries a fellow traveler toward a desired destination, a journey the coach has already taken, and often many
times. Aware of the potholes in life, a coach can guide this
fellow traveler around these often-unseen dangers. Had the
traveler walked this path alone, they may have unwearyingly
stepped into one of these deep holes, and figuratively speaking,
twisted an ankle or broken a leg.

I would never want to suggest that my experience or my
journey to healing was more painful or challenging than any
other fellow traveler. However, it was sufficient to create the
need for a better and deeper understanding of the topic and
the creation of a clear plan for healing.

As both a traveler and now a coach, I am excited to share
what I've learned on this journey. It is my desire to hasten your
healing and assist you in avoiding unnecessary pitfalls.

Glean as you read, select the parts that uniquely fit your
life. Embrace the principles and take the actions needed. And
may these principles serve you as they have so faithfully served
thousands of my coaching clients—and me.

Heir to the Chair

I have surrendered my free will to the years of accumulated habits and the past deeds of my life have already marked out a path which threatens to imprison my future.

— OG MANDINO

As HUMANS, we have been given a unique gift, the ability to step back and become aware of our unhealthy habits of thinking—we can *become* the Observer of our thoughts. This is called metacognition. Unlike all other living creatures on this planet, we can also change the way we think and choose to live above and beyond these damaging habits. We can choose to sit in the Observer's Chair.

Have a seat in the Observer's Chair. Firmly grip the arm-rests and hold them tightly. When we choose to sit here in *this* chair, we are full participants in life. We are whole and complete, confident, valiant, peaceful, deliberate, and unconditional with our self. Reflecting on the needs of others we are empathetic, respectful, accepting, tolerant, just and fair, and compassionate.

This is the place where we receive inspired ideas, impressions, and solutions to challenges—whispers and visions of possibility that ignite our passion and drive our focus, discipline, effort, and action. It is here that we act on our own moral authority doing the next right thing for the right reason because we want to, get to, and choose to. It is here that we find joy in the journey.

It is here that we experience success, happiness, and peace of mind. Yes, it is here that we learn, apply, and master the principles, practices, and processes that define the Observer—the one who consciously chooses to be an intentional creator.

This is a very good place. We know this chair. It feels like home, because when we choose to sit here, we are embracing our gifts and proactively choosing our destiny. After all, we are the Observer.

Notice the chair that is about ten feet in front of us. This is the chair of our unhealthy habits of thinking. When we choose to sit in *that* chair our unhealthy habits question our worth and worthiness, doubt our ability and challenge our beliefs and values.

This is where unrealistic expectations are created that foster fear and frustration. This is operation central, the home base for judgment and intolerance, despair and discouragement, overwhelm, and confusion. This is where we feel intimidated, exhausted, impatient, and disorganized.

This is where our unhealthy habits of thinking resist, resent, and even rebel against discipline and structure, goodness and light. Sitting in *that* chair over there, overwhelmed by the incessant noise, we cannot hear divine whispers or see visions of possibility.

In *that* chair over there, our efforts are sabotaged and we are stripped of our freedom and robbed of our hopes and dreams. This is a very dark place. Sadly, we also know *that* chair all too well.

When we move from the Observer's Chair—our chair—to the chair that belongs to our unhealthy habits of thinking, we surrender our free will—our right to make good choices and wise decisions. We also give up our voice. Yes, we turn our life and voice over to these habits. They are in charge—they run our life—they speak for us.

When we make the choice to sit in *that* chair over there, we do some crazy things and these *deeds* truly do threaten to imprison our future. Relationships suffer, productivity is impeded, confusion, and even anger abound—joy is elusive.

The operative question at any given moment in the day must always be, "In which chair am I choosing to sit? Am I in *this* chair—my chair—or have I moved over to *that* chair over there—the chair of my unhealthy habits of thinking?"

That chair over there can sometimes feel comfortable—at least familiar. It did for me—until I fully understood the price it was exacting from my self-esteem.

The Comparison Game

Vain attempts to imitate others no longer will I make. Instead will I place my uniqueness on display in the market place. I will proclaim it, yea, I will sell it. I will begin now to accent my differences; hide my similarities. So too will I apply this principle to the goods I sell. Salesman and goods, different from all others, and proud of the difference. I am a unique creature of nature. I am nature's greatest miracle.

— Og Mandino

No matter how loud, obnoxious, sabotaging or destructive our internal dialogue, no matter what our thoughts may want us to believe, no matter what we have done or what has been done to us, we are priceless and unique—we are nature's greatest miracle—we are the Observer.

I often reflect on the words of Robert S. Hartman, Ph.D., who created the formal axiological mathematics used in our Intentional Creation Assessment (see Appendix for more information).

He writes:

Unless you feel that you are of importance, nothing can be important to you. You must feel that you are important. You must take yourself seriously. If you take yourself as an accident that just as well might not have happened, if you dislike your own self, then you are lost. You are a loss to the universe. You cannot enrich the world. You have been created to enrich the world.

One of the great destroyers of self-esteem is the comparison game. Here we stand holding *our* clay—our greatest gifts, our greatest challenges—our current and unique life and life circumstances—our clay. Where is our focus? Do we want the clay we have been given? Do we want to create the most we can with our clay, or do we want someone else's clay? When we want someone else's we are trapped in *that* chair over there. I wanted someone else's. I was trapped.

When I stood holding my clay while reflecting on my childhood, I felt broken, unworthy, and incapable. Later in life when I stood holding my clay while reflecting on the loss of our material wealth, I felt paralyzed wanting to go back to *happier days* in an attempt to reclaim the clay I believed was lost.

How are we holding our clay? Do we want some *thing* we have never had and longed to receive, believing our happiness is contingent on having it? Do we embrace and honor and fully maximize our greatest gifts or do we minimize the value of these gifts wanting something more or different? Have we become our "stuff" or has the loss of stuff or lack of stuff left us feeling less than?

Where are we sitting? On what are we focused? Is it on creation or comparison—the Observer's Chair or the chair of our unhealthy habits of thinking?

In our media and image-driven society it is easy to engage in the *if only* comparison game—if only I had his or her body, hair, wardrobe, car, home—*if only* I had more education, money, or intelligence—*if only* I had a more interesting career—better health, a different companion, more obedient children, better family lineage, more luck—*if only's* in ad nauseum.

As we compare what we *have* versus what we *want* to have, we may become jealous of others. We may begin to minimize or devalue our ability—skills, natural talents, education or lack thereof—and look inward while asking, "Why am I so lacking?"

We may question the value of our tangible possessions, appearance and accomplishments. We may begin to sacrifice our time, energy, and even our well being in an attempt to prove our value. In the extreme, we may begin to feel resigned and hopeless and start wondering what it might be like on this planet without us here.

We may not plan suicide, but we would be okay if we got in an accident and died or could drive into that telephone pole or cement wall and have our cause of death ruled an accident.

When playing the comparison game, it is not uncommon

for us to take ten amazing people, select their best qualities, create one super human and then beat our self up for not stacking up.

On the other side of the coin and in an attempt to compensate for our lack, we may overemphasize the value of our possessions, ideas, beliefs, and opinions. We may even look for weaknesses in another's clay in an attempt to feel better about our own. We may say, "At least I'm not (this or that)." Or, "At least I haven't done (this or that)."

We talk about being independent and wanting to be our own person, yet far too often when we engage in the comparison game, we want to be someone else, somewhere else, doing something different—I did. When I focused on another person's clay, wanting what they had, I was imprisoned in *that* chair over there, chained down to my feelings of being less than.

When we are stuck in the chair of our unhealthy habits of thinking, letting go of comparison can be, as one client recently wrote, "like asking me not to breathe."

The truth? The day I chose to own my clay was the day I started breathing. This can be true for you, too.

Love Thy Self

Self-love is about having reverence for the infinite and intrinsic gift of life starting with our own clay. It is about honoring and magnifying our gifts—creating the most we can with what we have been given. It is about honoring our beliefs and embracing our intrinsic goodness. It is about being real, genuine, and authentic, free of doubt and fear, fully available to focus on and serve others—being the Observer.

In his writings, Dr. Hartman concluded that, *"Liking oneself is not an easy matter. In truth, philosophers have tried to give a method of how to do this from Socrates to Kierkegaard."* If a healthy self-esteem requires that we first love ourselves unconditionally and intrinsically, and it does, Dr. Hartman suggests that there are four critical steps we will want to embrace: Know Thyself, Choose Thyself, Create Thyself and Give Thyself.

Know Thyself

We will all want to engage in a truthful and introspective inventory of our life—past and present. We will also want to identify our gifts, talents, and the current condition of our finances, relationships, physical health, and spiritual lives. We will want to examine our failures and successes, our hurts and victories.

Take courage. For good or for ill, we do not create unfavorable life circumstances by looking at them; we just shed light on them and put them in proper perspective. When we shed light on our lives, we experience one of the great miracles of life—we somehow know what is good and we also know what needs to be changed. We also discover that we are inherently and intrinsically good—after all this is the gift given to an Observer.

Choose Thyself

Once we have identified our life experiences and the kind of person we have been and the assets with which we have to work, we will want to choose our *self*—warts and all. This is the clay we have been given to work with, the gifts and circumstances with which we can begin to build our new life.

Og encourages us with these words:

> *To grow and multiply it is necessary to plant the wheat grain in the darkness of the earth and my failures, my despairs, my ignorance, and my inabilities are the darkness in which I have been planted in order to ripen. Now, like the wheat grain which will sprout and blossom only if it is nurtured with rain and sun and warm winds, I too must nurture my body and mind to fulfill my dreams. But to grow to full stature the wheat must wait on the whims of nature. I need not wait for I have the power to choose my own destiny. Today I will multiply my value a hundredfold.*

These are the experiences that have shaped our character. These are the experiences that have heightened our empathy. These are the experiences we use to better understand what others are experiencing. These are reference points that help us better serve others. We will want to engrave these experiences on our hearts—own them. These experiences are one of the most valuable parts of our clay.

We cannot build our lives on a false premise. When we get real about our life, it may seem like there are no limits to the depths we must go in order to find bedrock on which to build. Dr. Hartman writes, *"But no matter how despicable you are to yourself you must choose yourself, accept yourself as the one you are. I am the one I am."*

This is the truth, for now, but it will not always be so. This is the foundation on which we can begin to build our new life and there is no ceiling to the growth that can be achieved when we choose to sit in the Observer's Chair and we start building from this rock-solid foundation. This is true no matter how deep we must dig to find bedrock.

Instead of investing our life living in resentment because of what we do not have, from here—the Observer's Chair—we shift our focus to creating the most we can with what we have been given—what *is!* Is our clay really that bad or only when compared to the clay of others or with the measuring rod of unrealistic expectations? It's time to get grounded.

When we choose our own clay, we honor the gift. When we focus on creating the most we can with our clay, we honor the Giver of the gift. This is how we can be grateful for what we have and still want more.

In truth, we are supposed to want more. We have been entrusted with this clay and have a fiduciary responsibility for creating the most we can with the clay we have been given. As an unknown author has written, *"Your life is a gift from God. What you choose to do with it is your gift to God."*

Until now we may have wanted to create our life using

someone else's clay—not possible. Until now, we may have been trying to keep one foot in fantasy and the other in reality and somehow create our dreams—not possible. Let us get focused and take action on the one thing that changes everything—owning our clay.

Lastly, when we choose our clay, we do not give up anything of true value or give in to any weakness. We just stop trying to be someone else and give up all the accompanying resistance, resentment, and rebellion. Let us choose our clay. This pivotal decision alone can have a huge impact on healing our self-esteem.

Create Thyself

Let's rise early each day committed to create the most we can with the clay we have been given. Let's focus on the lessons learned and how these challenges have provided opportunities for more growth. Let's commit to stretch and grow and become the person who can handle increasing levels of stress with greater and greater levels of ease. Let's plug into the planet.

Again, Og provides inspiration:

I have been given eyes to see and a mind to think and now I know a great secret of life for I perceive, at last, that all my problems, discouragements, and heartaches are, in truth, great opportunities in disguise. I will no longer be fooled by the garments they wear for mine eyes are open. I will look beyond the cloth and I will not be deceived.

Here is another secret of success. As we create the most we can with the clay we have been given, as a bonus, we not only experience increasing levels of success—we are also given more clay. This only happens when we fully maximize the value of the gifts already given. After all, why would the Giver of clay give more clay to someone who devalues the clay they have already been given? Herein we find the foundational principle of abundance—magnifying our talents.

As Intentional Creation commences, we focus all of our energy on making the most we can with our clay and not on our lack of clay. Miracles begin to unfold. Dr. Hartman writes, *"You must start as early as you can, but it is never too late."*

Give Thyself

The more honest and transparent we become with our self, the more we are able to get out of our own way. We grow unfettered by fear and shame or the need to compare. Our cup is filled and begins to run over—we have more and enough to spare. We give of our self freely and are fed instead of feeling depleted.

Dr. Hartman writes, *"This means, forget all limitations, be generous with your own self. Give your own self to your fellow man and to the world. Love your neighbor as yourself. Throw your bread on the water."* It is in the giving of our self to others that we finally find our true self, our true worth. Our pain and suffering finally have meaning and purpose. We want *our* clay. It's here that we find joy.

When we have the courage to dig deep and know our self, and then choose our self, and then create the most we can with the clay we have been given, we tap into an infinite supply of power, a veritable treasure chest. We find our real gifts and with them the power to love our self and thus, love others more fully. Our cup can be overflowing, but only when we choose to sit in the Observer's Chair.

This is a great secret. Prior to this exercise, we may have been looking for love in all the wrong places.

Unmet Expectations

My dreams are worthless, my plans are dust, my goals are impossible. All are of no value unless they are followed by action. I will act now.

— Og Mandino

THE INTENTIONAL CREATION of our dreams occurs in two very different yet equally important dimensions, first, in our mind, and second, in the physical world. We engage in mental creation using the essential and very powerful gift of vivid visualization.

Challenges with self-esteem occur when we choose to move to *that* chair over there and allow this gift to be used destructively. The most common destructive uses of vivid visualization include: escape and avoid fantasy, fatigue-driven pessimism, obligation, the need to be right, and counterfeit forms of pleasure.

When our secret desires and real intentions are focused on

a life of ease and comfort, or arrival, and life keeps showing up differently, these destructive uses of this gift are the natural default. When we want a more exotic life and we seek counterfeit forms of pleasure such as pornography, we can also become slaves to these damaging thoughts.

The more difficult or mundane our life circumstances, the more likely we are to be captured by these destructive habits of thinking—the more likely we are to unconsciously surrender our free will to *that* chair over there.

Escape and Avoid Fantasy

When we experience a traumatic event or series of events that are beyond our ability to understand, comprehend or control, we may develop coping skills that assist us in surviving. We may venture out *there* just long enough to get a job done while attempting to appear normal, but never long enough to get hurt again.

The most effective coping skill I found as a child was escaping into my mind. Here I was safe and in control. As one peer said while commiserating, "Growing up, some of my favorite people were imaginary characters." So true.

If we have experienced a traumatic event, it is quite normal to have developed a very vivid imagination. It is also not too difficult to connect the dots between the creation of this imagination and a natural default to engage in escape and avoid fantasy. Back then it was all about safety. Now it is all about ease and comfort and a less stressful life.

We need not have a traumatic event in order to surrender to this unhealthy habit. We may simply be struggling with the current firestorms of life. In today's economy these challenges can at times seem merciless. Seeking relief, we may be tempted to engage in escape and avoid fantasy simply to get away from these heavy burdens. It is so easy to do. It is so euphoric when we go over there and sit in *that* chair and indulge.

Others may not fully appreciate the relationship between effort and results and want to believe there is an easy way. They want to believe there is a fantasy fairy that will magically manifest their wishes in tangible reality if they but visualize their dreams with enough intention. There are more than a few out there trying to sell easy buttons. Have you ever tried to buy one? If so, you too have felt buyer's remorse.

Whether it be traumatic events, firestorms, or the pursuit of ease that drives the desire to escape and avoid, when we engage in fantasy, we commence a journey of no return that can destroy self-esteem.

We start by traveling in our mind to a future event or desired outcome. We then begin playing out vivid visual scenarios as if this event or outcome has already occurred.

The vividness, with which many are capable of visualizing, triggers the same brain chemistry and brain circuitry involved with the actual activity. The brain creates what neuroscientists call a Mental Construct—we have constructed a new reality in our mind. The brain believes the fantasy is real. Our body responds with feelings of euphoria and sometimes even tears of joy.

While in fantasy, we can visualize an early evening flight to France on our private jet, two weeks in the Caribbean sunbathing and scuba diving. We can purchase and decorate our luxuriant oceanfront home in Malibu and buy a tropical island in the Pacific. We can pay off our parents' mortgage, buy new cars for our siblings, and donate millions to worthy causes.

On the other hand, we can simply use this gift to vividly visualize a life of ease and comfort—free of debt and stress. And, we can do all of this in the fifteen minutes it takes to shower, each vivid scenario created mentally in a nanosecond.

Not only have we skipped past all the work required to create this outcome, we have now created an expectation—a nonnegotiable mental monolith—a concrete condition for happiness—a yardstick by which reality is measured and valued.

What are the chances that reality will show up different than our fantasy? What happens when it does? Quoting from my first book, *Today I Begin a New Life*, here is a haunting description:

> *When we fantasize, we commence a dangerous journey that quickly and cruelly turns from euphoria to a ghoulish nightmare—an undulating and deadly rollercoaster of emotions.*
>
> *First, the sympathetic nervous system releases the powerful drug norepinephrine, so powerful that if it were a*

prescribed drug, it would be a controlled substance. We feel euphoric, wonderful, emotionally high...I call this artificial or counterfeit joy.

Within twenty-four hours, tangible reality shows up differently—and it always does—threatening our new reality. Suddenly it's as if we're being attacked by a grizzly bear.

The mind and body immediately engage in a violent, defensive battle. This reaction is autonomic, meaning we cannot control it. Instead of joy, we feel a lightning bolt of anxiety and fear as our sympathetic nervous system releases the antithesis of a euphoric drug—a large and often chronic dose of cortisol.

Our hippocampus, which supports short-term memory, locks down like a bank vault—nothing in, nothing out. Adding insult to injury, the amygdala, the flight or fight center of the brain, sends out an army of fear dendrites to shut down energy-rich portions of our brain, starting with the prefrontal cortex.

As a result, our higher levels of consciousness, empathy and practical judgment—people skills and common sense—are rendered impotent. The mind and body are preparing for one singular agenda—war.

The cortisol is designed to speed up metabolism and heal wounds, but who is the enemy? The fear dendrites have preserved the energy needed for fight or flight, but where do we direct this energy? Who are we supposed to fight? Is it a raging bear or some other fierce adversary?

No, it's simply reality attacking our expectations, our concrete conditions for happiness, those giant, non-negotiable mental monoliths. When this occurs, those closest to us may at times feel like we are the enemy.

As seductive and euphoric as fantasy can be, in the end, it fosters only fear, and ultimately, disease. It will never create tangible reality. Fantasy violates every principle of creation. Again, it seeks to avoid the very work of creation.

When we engage in fantasy, we inevitably experience discouragement, overwhelm, frustration, impatience, and even anger—the antithesis of inspiration and passion. We may engage in frenetic non-goal-related activities when linear time does not keep pace, which it can't—busy, busy, busy, always busy, always exhausted, never sure of what we have accomplished.

We may spend valuable hours worrying—playing out endless worst-case scenarios and tormenting our self over events that may never come to pass. We may stand on the rim of a metaphorical canyon, having vividly visited the other side, and be left feeling desperate in the search for a way to bridge the chasm. We may begin to discount the value of what we have and what we are doing and long for greener pastures or an easier way.

We may begin to focus on our *lack*, starting with a lack of worth and worthiness. We may begin to play out endless examples of past errors—past mistakes—such as lapses in judgment, moments of greed, flashes of weakness while trying to identify the reasons for our current failures or unanswered prayers.

We may begin to question if we have the ability to create our dreams. We may begin to question our core ideals and beliefs or believe we must sacrifice or compromise these beliefs if we are to get what we want. We can become resistant, resentful, defensive, and angry.

We may exclaim, as did a new client years ago, "I can almost touch it. I can almost taste it. Why can't I have it?" Unable to find the answers, most turn inward and ask, "What is wrong with me?" In the extreme, we may ask, "Does God not love me?"

While sitting in the chair of our unhealthy habits of thinking, have we ever found our self trapped in this emotional rollercoaster—norepinephrine-driven emotional highs followed by cortisol and fear dendrite-driven emotional lows?

I sure got a few bruises from my wild undulating trips around these tracks. There were times when it made me want to throw up. So how can we get off this crazy carnival ride?

I shared the following in my book, *Today I Begin a New Life.*

When we spend productive time in these castles in the sky, we are losing and even wasting the time needed to create worthy dreams in tangible reality. Henry David Thoreau wisely counsels, "If you have built castles in the sky, you need not be lost; that is where they should be. Now put foundations underneath them."

All is not lost. The good news is this! We have the gift of vivid visualization—we can see possibilities! Now let us see in a way that manifests inspired ideas, impressions, and solutions to challenges that can ignite our passion and drive our actions.

I remember well the morning in Sacramento when I was sharing this deadly sequence—creating unrealistic expectations, experiencing frustration when life shows up differently, and the human tendency to turn inward looking for self-blame—to a fun group of eager participants in a workshop. Suddenly in the back of the room, on my right side, a young man began to enthusiastically wave his hand. A light had clearly turned on. I acknowledged him.

He stood and shared that he had good parents and a great childhood. There were no apparent reasons why his self-esteem should be "in the toilet" but it was. "I finally get it," he exclaimed. He went on to share how he had been investing productive hours during the day escaping into the future and then vividly visualizing what it would be like then.

"I just wanted my dreams to be magically manifest. When that didn't happen I thought something was wrong with me and I beat myself up."

For the first time he connected the dots between his dreams

and doing the work of creation. He finally realized that everything beyond the dream was contingent on first creating the dream. He had wanted to prematurely experience the benefits from something he had not yet created. It was here that he would want to focus his energy—on the millimeters of creation—and this could only be accomplished while sitting in the Observer's Chair.

There was nothing wrong with him or us. We are simply sitting in the wrong chair. All we have to do is stand up and move over and learn how to use our gift of vivid visualization constructively. In doing so, we immediately begin to experience the benefits—inspired ideas, impressions and solutions to challenges that ignite passion and drive action.

True, staying here in the Observer's Chair will require some diligence; after all, fantasy is alluring. Now we know better than to engage. A few moments of euphoria are never worth the thrashing. Our self-esteem deserves better.

Fatigue-Driven Pessimism

Over the past four years, starting in early 2009, I began to notice an increase in the severity of unhealthy habits of thinking that negatively impact self-esteem. This was true especially for those who previously used their gift of vivid visualization constructively—clear vision, immediate, deliberate, intentional and sustained action, results.

The evidence of the problem began to manifest in a

Characteristic of Mental Creation entitled, Pragmatic. This measurement started to reveal significant levels of overwhelm. This measurement had been balanced the majority of the time with those who were natural intentional creators, but no longer. Not surprising, this phenomenon coincided with the economic downturn.

For many, the growth of their businesses had slowed dramatically, if not contracted. The expectations created after years of employment, investment, dedication and hard work—job security, stable and sustained cash flow, equity or asset growth, and desired time and financial freedom—were being shattered. Faced with the prospect of re-engaging at previous levels of activity in order to save or rebuild a business or starting over somewhere else was both frightening and overwhelming.

The last time they climbed up this ladder, they were driven by passion. They were in creation mode. They worked without counting the costs or tracking the time. They willingly washed the windows and took out the trash—whatever was required.

They had a vision and were determined to make it happen. They did not want to live in fantasy. They never sought ease. They wanted real money, in a real bank account, which could buy a real couch. And create they did.

Looking back and in truth, if they had known beforehand what would have been required and how it would turn out, many reported, "I would have chosen a different ladder." However, vision and the resultant passion had provided a deep reservoir of sustained energy needed to climb.

Now standing on the shrinking bedrock of reality and while looking up at where they want to be or used to be, fully aware this time of what is required to climb, they are overwhelmed by e v e r y t h i n g that needs to be done—every rung in the ladder.

It is not uncommon to hear from these exhausted pioneers of business, "I don't know if I have the strength to do it again." The truth is, they won't—unless they can again find ways to re-ignite their passion. And passion can only be accessed while sitting in the Observer's Chair.

Absent this passion and while mired in the chair of un-healthy habits, the harm done to self-esteem is and will continue to be very similar to that of a person who engages in fantasy, but with this one exception. Instead of questioning or doubting talent or ability, the doubt is focused on being able to sustain the effort required.

As exhaustion continues to mount, I often hear, "I don't know how much longer I can keep doing this." Those struggling with fatigue will want to stand, walk away from this self-defeating dialogue, move over to the Observer's Chair, and learn how to ignite passion. If you are one of them, you know what it feels like to sit in this chair. Jump back in. It is a lot more fulfilling to work from here.

Obligation

When fatigue settles in, we can shift to obligation-based motivation. Instead of doing things because we want to, get to and choose to, we do things because we have to, need to, should, and must. In the extreme, we can do things out of a fear of consequences—what will happen if I don't do it.

When our underlying driver is obligation, we start the day by strapping on a metaphorical backpack full of bricks. Anyone know the names of these bricks of obligation?

Backpack strapped on, we run just as fast, but are heavily burdened. Inescapably we get tired. When we reach the point where we are so exhausted that we can't take it any longer, we rebel.

Rebellion shows up differently for everyone. Some get irritated or angry. Others become reclusive. Others simply avoid the issues by escaping into a more pleasant activity.

While in rebellion we may consider the possibilities of quitting. When most people think about it, they quickly shift into guilt for ever having considered it—"So many people are depending on me. I can't quit. I have to keep going."

So, we pull our self up by the bootstraps and re-commit, but commit to what? We go back and do what we have to, need to, should, and must—our obligations—until we get tired and the cycle begins all over again.

Self-esteem is damaged when we begin to believe that we must sacrifice our time, energy and even our well-being to serve everyone else—we have no other options—we have to, need to, should, and must. Sometimes it's the sheer volume of our commitments that is so exhausting—we may have a challenge saying, "No!" After all, our ability and thus our worth is on the line. However, a great deal of the time, exhaustion comes simply by how we hold our commitments—*have to* versus *want to*.

Obligation can become even more damaging to self-esteem when our unhealthy habits convince us that no matter what we do it is never good enough. If this is ringing a bell, where did *this* unhealthy habit come from? At one time in our life, was this unhealthy habit the voice of another person? It's difficult to feel whole and complete, capable and valuable when our thoughts are unrelenting and unyielding in their pursuit of the unachievable—perfection-driven.

Healing can come with a more structured calendar that includes downtime—me time. It can also come from a fundamental shift in motivation from obligation to self-direction—acting on our own moral authority, doing the next right thing for the right reason because we want to, get to, and choose to. It can also come in a shift from perfection to excellence. As Mark LeBlanc says, "Better done than perfect."

The Need to Be Right

How active are our minds? How much time do we spend thinking about thinking? What happens when we put a few drops of negativity in this giant caldron? What happens when we get attached to an idea?

Our research uncovered a poignant fact. Over 95% plus of the population cannot separate their ideas from their self-worth. Ideas and worth are inextricably connected.

To better understand the power in this discovery, take your two hands, palms together, fingers intertwined. Now squeeze your hands together tightly. Your right hand represents a person's self-esteem and the left hand represents that person's ideas.

In the vast majority of the population, these two concepts cannot be separated. When we disagree with a person's ideas, we negatively impact that person's self-esteem. The same is true in reverse. When someone does not agree with us, it can impact our self-esteem.

The obsessive thoughts that drive this process are called systemic thoughts. Unlike any other thought, systemic thoughts process dualistically—right/wrong, win/lose, all/nothing, life/death. When we obsessively think, we construct ideas in our mind and we get attached to these ideas. Once built, an idea is no longer just an idea—it's a done deal—life or death.

To further complicate this challenge, we may not only need to be right, we may know we *are* right. Being aware of these right/wrong, win/lose systemic thoughts in moments like these absolutely requires us being firmly planted in the Observer's Chair.

When we feel strongly about an idea, we want to step back

and consider, "I'm right, but so what if I'm right? I do not want to crush a human being over this." From the unique vantage point of the Observer's Chair, we can see this person's uniqueness and value. To override the need to be right, we will want to have this level of awareness. We can be right or we can be rich. We choose to be rich in terms of our relationships and our finances.

So what happens if we are unconscious in these right/wrong moments and we surrender to *that* chair over there? Let's watch it unfold.

We get into a conversation with someone who needs to be right about an idea or approach to something. We feel strongly about a different approach. We start pushing the other person's buttons and the other person starts pushing ours. One of two things happen:

1. A right/wrong battle ensues. Just as soon as the battle begins, the focus shifts. It's no longer about the topic at hand. It is now about the preservation of self-esteem.

    To protect self-esteem, the fight continues. We might be thinking, "Why can't they see how ridiculous that position is?!" They are thinking the same thing. There is no compromise so anger rages. Harsh words are spoken.

    Our obsessive thought processes have invested heavily in our idea. They have explored every option, and in our opinion, we have the best solution. It is as if the other person is calling into question our worth and worthiness, our ability, and even our beliefs and opinions. How dare they? This is personal. In the end, feelings get hurt and frustration abounds. And when the dust settles, damage control is required.

2. We let the person win. We are either tired of fighting, want to belong, or want to keep the peace. This decision does not come without damage. We experience private, painful feelings of personal sacrifice.

Here is the last piece to this complex puzzle. When we need to be right and someone is pushing our buttons—calling into question our worth—we are fighting to protect our self from the same dialogue that our unhealthy habits speak to us privately. Ouch! No wonder we are so sensitive.

What is the answer? Get over in the Observer's Chair as quickly as possible and take a seat! Here we can extricate our self from the shadow side of these systemic thoughts—the need to be right—and see the value in a human being.

Sitting over here, we choose to find good in a person's idea. We don't need to agree with them, but we can always find good in their idea. When we do this, the person feels validated, walls come down, and cooperation floods out.

When discussing this principle with a new client, I shared that systemic thoughts cannot distinguish the seriousness of the topic at hand—they need to be right about everything. I then smiled and shared that if we are not careful we can risk blowing apart a marriage based on the correct topping for a pizza—pepperoni or sausage. She laughed and said, "No, actually it was a bagel." We both chuckled, but in truth it is seldom funny in the heat of a battle.

Footnote: All is now well in her home. And of course, I'm so glad I have never struggled with this challenge. Ramona, is that you chuckling?

Counterfeit Pleasure

The most common form of counterfeit pleasure is the habit of viewing pornography. We can strive to protect first amendment rights for others, but we can also choose to make wise decisions about our own behaviors. I have witnessed first hand and on numerous occasions the devastating impact that pornography can have on self-esteem.

Individually, it negatively impacts our ability to have agape love and authentically connect with others. Instead of valuing the sanctity of human life, it objectifies human beings. It promotes destructive fantasies that artificially create arousal and self-centric satisfaction, which in turn counterfeits heightened feelings reserved for intimacy—intimacy that is focused on meeting the needs of a partner. It can also drive a person deep into an emotional cocoon, supporting reclusive tendencies and isolating a person from reality. It destroys self-trust.

In relationships, this unhealthy habit is one of the greatest destroyers of self-esteem. It impedes true intimacy—the ultimate expression of commitment and trust—by bringing these salacious fantasies into the sacred space of union. A partner can intuit when someone's mind is somewhere else. Questions of personal beauty and ultimately self-worth are unavoidable.

This is only exacerbated should a partner discover the source. I have heard women cry out, "Why am I not enough?" This is often followed by a litany of possible reasons, most of which are focused on concerns about their outward appearance. The comparison game is common even without this challenge, but when someone discovers that a partner is engaged in pornography it raises this self-deprecating dialogue to dangerous and heart-breaking levels.

If we only knew the full impact that this unhealthy habit can have on the self-esteem of our partner, we would more consciously choose to stand and move over here to the Observer's Chair. Here we would never debase a human being. We would be empathetic. We would possess a deep and profound reverence for the infinite worth of every human being. We would value each person as unique and irreplaceable—including our self.

If we are struggling with pornography—measured by making promises to our self or others to abstain and then breaking those promises—it's time for professional intervention. Here is the truth. Until harmful habits such as this one are pruned off we cannot expect our soul to be whole and complete and our relationship to become a partnership. Everything about pornography is antithetical to healing self-esteem.

Summary

Interestingly, in those actively seeking success, the two thought processes that determine the frequency, level of obsession, and the vividness with which a person visualizes, are both significantly over-focused 97% of the time. Simply stated, we spend inordinate amounts of time thinking about thinking. Our mind is almost always somewhere else. Far too often it is stuck in the chair of our unhealthy habits of thinking.

Destructive uses of this gift constitute some of the toughest habits to break primarily because they relegate us to the deepest dungeons of despair and discouragement. And the damage to self-esteem is significant.

Let's break out the tomahawk of choice and chop the air while saying, "I'm not going to *that* chair over there today. I am staying in the Observer's Chair." Repeat if needed.

Here we focus on being self-directed, honorable, goal-oriented, coachable, pragmatic, and resolute. No more fantasizing. No more pessimistic thinking. No more obligatory motivations. No more salacious mental movies.

Over here in the Observer's Chair, we focus on connecting, serving, creating value, and contributing to the world. We use our gift of vivid visualization constructively.

Instead of racing off into the distant future to a time when all is well, we mentally rehearse important near-term events seeking clear direction while asking, "What can I create? How can I create it? How will that serve?" We ask, "If there is anyone

I can serve, put them on my path," and we receive inspiration. We explore possibilities before making tangible commitments and minimize mistakes. We give our mind solvable problems to contemplate. We put together a plan and set goals for both our personal relationships and our businesses. In short, we think constructively.

In so doing, inspired ideas, impressions, and solutions to challenges are manifest. We hear these whispers and visions of possibility and our passion is ignited. Passion drives our focus, discipline, effort and action. We stay present, living in the NOW, maximizing our gifts. We know who we are and are known. We trust and can be trusted. Our self-esteem has a safe place in which to heal.

Note: The five constructive ways of thinking briefly outlined above are discussed in great detail in my first book, *Today I Begin a New Life.*

Damaged Trust

I will waste not a moment mourning yesterday's misfortunes, yesterday's defeats, yesterday's aches of the heart, for why should I throw good after bad? I will live this day as if it is my last.

— Og Mandino

WE HAVE ALL heard the statement, "Go to the light." It has never been truer than when we are sitting in the dark chair of our unhealthy habits of thinking, with our trust in humanity damaged, feeling alone and afraid.

Imprisoned by traumatic events that damaged the fragile underpinnings of trust, we may have become fearful, cautious or even reclusive. We may have been unable or unwilling to let go and move forward or even believe it's possible.

Due to these events, we may have become attached to our unhealthy habits of thinking—the ones that question our worth and worthiness—the ones that want us to retrospectively assign to our childhood memories the wisdom and decision making ability of a mature adult—the ones that want us to second guess our every financial or relationship decision and doubt our ability to think clearly or act appropriately—the ones that talk us out of confronting unacceptable or aberrant conduct—the ones that want us to take responsibility for another person's poor judgment, poor performance or harmful behavior—the ones that tell us we should have known better, listened more intently, been wiser, got out sooner, been more responsible, acted differently.

You are nature's greatest miracle. Stand up and move to the light—the Observer's Chair. It is here, embracing our real voice, that we can find wholeness and the peace of mind for which we hunger.

The most common examples of traumatic events include:

- A lack of proper nurturing during developmental years
- Feelings of abandonment when parents separate or divorce
- Emotional, physical or sexual abuse experienced as a child or as an adult
- Infidelity (emotional and physical) on the part of a committed companion or spouse
- Divorce or separation
- Unexpected or untimely job loss
- Serious financial setbacks due to circumstances out of our control

Some survive these events seemingly unscathed while others experience deep wounds that leave painful debilitating scars. Some may need assistance from a skilled therapist to process through these traumas.

Come on a little journey with me to three pivotal moments that helped facilitate my healing. Together let's find meaning and purpose that can serve you.

The Treasure Chest

At six, I was given a tender mercy. It signaled the beginning of my journey back to wholeness. At the time, we lived in a small town a few miles away from the Thiokol solid fuel rocket test plant where my father worked. One night, while sound asleep, I had a vivid dream.

In the dream, I sneaked out of the back door of our house, down the concrete steps and out onto the lawn. Even though it was night, I could see clearly. I had a shovel in my hand and an overwhelming feeling that a treasure was buried somewhere in my backyard. I remember being very excited.

I felt drawn to a specific spot and began to dig. About three feet down, I hit something hard. Clearing away the dirt, I found the lid to a large metal box. I opened it and peeked inside. Much to my delight, it was filled to overflowing with mounds and mounds of shiny, silver quarters. I dug my hands into the treasure and let the booty stream through my open fingers. I did it again and again, each time digging deeper and deeper. The box seemed bottomless.

To a six-year-old coin collector, a single quarter was a really big deal. I had to pull weeds for a whole day to earn just one. This box in my backyard had thousands and thousands—tons more quarters than there were pennies in my Grandma Hansen's giant Log Cabin Syrup tin. I was rich beyond my wildest six-year-old imagination.

Over the years, I have revisited this dream many times. Even though I didn't fully understand it at the time, or fully appreciate its significance, the vivid images always lifted my soul and inspired me to keep moving forward.

Angels Among Us

At the age of nine we moved to Woodbine, Georgia. I attended White Oak Elementary. Even as a child, I found it interesting to attend a country school where old-fashioned wooden desks were bolted to the floor—*Little House on the Prairie* style—and the restroom was in a separate but adjoining building having been added years after the construction of the original school. We did have electricity.

I shall never forget my fifth-grade teacher, Ms. Virginia Colsen, an angel sent down from heaven. One day, Ms. Colsen was called out of the classroom. Her final words to us were, "Be good boys while I am gone." That lasted for about a minute. Soon a few were engaged in a friendly rubber-band fight. I held back and then decided to participate—fully. At that precise moment, Ms. Colsen returned. We were all caught red-handed.

Ms. Colsen stood pondering our punishment. Usually we would get a good swat administered by one of the male teachers or the vice-principal using one of their fraternity paddles. Today would be very different.

As Ms. Colsen scanned the room looking each boy in the eye, she finally spoke, "You will learn Rudyard Kipling's classic poem, *If.*" She paused for a moment and then added, "And, you will not be allowed to go outside for recess until you do so." Some of the guys would never again see the sun during a school day for the balance of that year.

That night, determined to be the first, a common overcompensation for those with challenged self-esteem and in need of recognition, I memorized the poem. The next day, I stood before the class and recited it.

Ms. Colsen was delighted. She took me by the hand and paraded me from classroom to classroom, giving me several more opportunities to do so. I share it now. Perhaps these words can speak to all of us as they spoke to me back then.

IF
by Rudyard Kipling

If you can keep your head when all about you
Are losing theirs and *blaming it on you,*
If you can trust yourself when *all men doubt you,*
But make allowance for their doubting too;
If you can wait and not be *tired by waiting,*

Or being lied about, don't deal in lies,
Or being hated, *don't give way to hating,*
And yet *don't look too good, nor talk too wise,*
If you can dream—and not make dreams your master;
If you can think—and not make thoughts your aim;
If you can meet with *Triumph and Disaster*
And treat those two impostors just the same;
If you can bear to *hear the truth you've spoken*
Twisted by knaves to make a trap for fools,
Or watch the things *you gave your life to, broken,*
And stoop and build 'em up with worn-out tools:
If you can make one heap of all your winnings
And risk it on one turn of pitch-and-toss,
And lose, and start again at your beginnings
And never breathe a word about your loss;
If you can force your heart and nerve and sinew
To serve your turn long after they are gone,
And so hold on when there is nothing in you
Except the Will which says to them: 'Hold on!'
If you can *talk with crowds and keep your virtue,*
Or walk with Kings—*nor lose the common touch,*
If neither foes nor loving friends can hurt you,
If all men count with you, but none too much;
If you can fill the unforgiving minute

With sixty seconds' worth of distance run,
Yours is the Earth and everything that's in it,
And—which is more—*you'll be a Man, my son*!

It was as if Ms. Colsen knew that I needed these words of encouragement. With them I got my first glimpse into the possibility of wholeness—what it could be like to sit in the Observer's Chair. I shall always love Ms. Colsen for loving me.

Who are the Ms. Colsens—the angels in your life—the ones that encouraged you to stretch and grow, the ones that showed up in the important moments when you needed a friend?

Chicago Dream

A little over four decades later, and after experiencing a few more trials, it was time for the most precious healing experience. While in Chicago to give a speech I had another vivid dream.

In this dream I was walking down a long narrow path. I was dragging a large white muslin sack over my right shoulder. It was heavy and I was exhausted. I saw a man approaching. A kind and gentle voice told me to stop, let go of the sack, turn around, empty the sack and examine the contents. Reluctant and fearful, I did as instructed.

As I held each item from my sack in my hands—each a symbol of a failure, an inability, a hurtful and harmful thing that had been done to me, or something I had done to hurt another—I was asked a simple question, "Is anyone else suffering from a similar wound?" With each item inspected, the answer was a resounding, "Yes!"

I was asked to take each experience and press it against my chest and engrave it on my heart. As I did so, a reassuring voice delivered a sweet and healing message I shall never forget:

> *David, your character has been forged in the furnace of adversity. You know what pain feels like. You cannot change the past. However, you can choose to use these experiences as reference points, a rich resource to assist you in better understanding, connecting with, and serving others. When you choose to use these life experiences in the service of others, you will finally find purpose in your past suffering, joy in your journey, and much-needed healing in your soul.*

After engraving these experiences on my heart, I was asked to turn around. I did as instructed and for the first time noticed that the man approaching me was also dragging a large white muslin sack. It was clear. I could not see his sack until I owned the contents of mine.

Having owned mine, I somehow knew what was in his sack—I could *feel* his pain. Intuitive impressions and empathetic questions floated effortlessly to the surface. When asked, these questions created understanding and connection.

Deeply buried treasures in our own backyard, angels in our life, dragging heavy sacks, choosing to hold our experiences—these treasures—in our heart, using this priceless gift as a lens through which we can more clearly see another person, connecting with and serving others. Could this be the secret to moving forward and healing?

When we choose to move forward, we choose to let go of the pain, guilt, shame, regrets, frustration, resentment, rebellion, jealousy, and anger caused by these experiences—all self-centric emotions. We engrave these experiences on our heart. I discovered that these experiences became my bridge to connection and to a new life. Perhaps you too have some painful experiences with which to build your bridge.

Moving Forward

When we choose to move forward with our life, we do not leave these life experiences behind. We take them with us. These are *our* experiences and we have paid dearly to get them. They have shaped and molded our character—our true self. These experiences have uniquely prepared us to more confidently stand on another person's path, more clearly see and understand the circumstances of their life and then serve them more effectively.

When we use our experiences this way, understanding prevails, trust is established, walls of resistance come down, and cooperation floods out. Ultimately, we are the beneficiaries. We discover that our experiences, good and difficult, are our greatest asset. They are the catalyst that helps create connection; connection that facilitates the release of unspeakable joy; the kind of joy that heals self-esteem.

Few have looked here for healing. It seems to be a well-kept secret. Let us share it with everyone who will listen.

Victimhood and Denial

Far too many waste valuable time turning inward searching for answers. While swimming in this dark and self-centric pool of ugly experiences, my questions always started with, "Why me?" I spent too many years lamenting and even resenting my life experiences. Nearly every breath was filled with should have, could have, and ought-to-have regrets.

We can remain stuck—mired and even drowning in the past. Burdened by the weight of our sack, we can struggle just to stay afloat, let alone move forward.

This is where I first went in search for answers—inside—but here I could find no peace of mind. In my book, *Today I Begin a New Life*, I wrote the following while reflecting on my own journey:

Have we ever had one of those times when we felt hurt and wanted people to know about it? How about a time when we worked hard, sacrificed, suffered, and wanted people to appreciate it? Perhaps we have experienced a very real physical, financial, spiritual, or emotional crisis?

When these experiences occur, we may be tempted to ask, "But if I empty my sack, engrave my experiences on my heart, show up okay, responsible, accountable, and ready to serve others, how will people know how much I have suffered? How will they know how hard I've worked and the sacrifices I've made?"

The truth is that some life challenges are really difficult. Some require a period of mourning, especially ones involving the loss of a loved one. But most challenges do not require mourning. When we choose to hang on to the past, we can quickly become a prisoner in the dark dungeons of despair and discouragement. We get stuck, and our heart becomes small and bitter.

Burdened by the heaviness of an overflowing sack, we may want people to feel sorry for us. We may even attempt to assign responsibility for our success and happiness to others. We may seek to be rescued. We can feel frustrated, angry, used, or abandoned. We may long to be understood. Our attempts to garner sympathy exhaust all—self and others— and we are left with an empty cup that can never be filled.

I could find no healing balm in this dark place of self-focus no matter how deep I dug or how many layers I peeled off the proverbial onion. It simply made my eyes water while my wounds remained open and festering.

Then I tried to move forward by letting go—forgetting all. It was as if chunks of my life never happened. After all, if we repent even God forgets, right? So why couldn't I forget? I just couldn't.

Again from personal experience, I wrote:

*Like me, so many have been taught at one time or an-
other, in one way or another, creative ways to release these
painful memories. Some are told to write these experiences
on a piece of paper and burn it. Others are told to write
their experiences on a rock and throw it out into the ocean.
Everyone agrees that it feels better for a moment or two,
but it does not take long and we are again standing in
sackcloth and ashes or watching as the tides of life wash
these painful memories back onto the rocky shores of life.*

*I wanted these wounds and crushing memories to belong
to another person—the old me. I wanted to be born anew,
free both from my sins and from these painful memories.
This lifelong struggle of forgiving and repenting, yet still
feeling connected to these memories had left me confused
and exhausted to the core.*

*Now I know that to erase these memories would be to
throw away something of great value, perhaps my single
greatest asset—the very source of my empathy—my ability
to place myself on another person's path and more clearly
see and understand what they are experiencing. Yes, I am
speaking of the value in my memories—even from the most
awful and painful life experiences.*

When we try to distance our self from our past experiences,
wanting these experiences to belong to another person, we lose

the richness in these lessons of life and the power that comes with ownership. Our heart remains self-focused and we live life anesthetized and unaware of the subtle needs of others.

We cannot live life to its fullest consigned to an anesthetized version of our self. With periodic and painful awakenings to the past, followed by the challenge of reconciling two different lives, I was left with the plaguing question, "Who am I, really?"

Agape Love

What a relief to discover—memories never die—they aren't supposed to. These experiences are the furnace in which our character has been forged. It is here that we have been uniquely prepared to better understand another person's similar challenges.

In Scroll II, *I will greet this day with love in my heart,* Og tells us that love—agape love—is the greatest secret in all ventures and with it we can melt all hearts like the sun whose rays soften the coldest clay.

Agape love references a state of mind—a heightened level of awareness. Agape love requires that we climb up and out of our personal agenda and baggage—our unhealthy habits of thinking—and sit in the chair of the Observer and see the bigger picture.

After sharing what agape love can do, Og then asks, "And how will I do this?"

Here is his answer:

Henceforth will I look on all things with [agape] love and I will be born again. I will love the sun for it warms my bones; yet I will love the rain for it cleanses my spirit. I will love the light for it shows me the way; yet I will love the darkness for it shows me the stars. I will welcome happiness for it enlarges my heart; yet I will endure sadness for it opens my soul. I will acknowledge rewards for they are my due; yet I will welcome obstacles for they are my challenge.

We discover that, when faced with life's challenges, agape love asks us to rise above the gravity of a given circumstance and find meaning and purpose. It asks us to show up more courageously and inspire others to do likewise.

When connecting with people, agape love asks us to look beyond our personal bias and prejudice—other unhealthy habits of thinking—and become aware of another person's needs, desires, hopes, dreams, fear, and pain. It asks us to create a safe place where there is no need for walls. Let's be found possessing agape love.

Summary

In truth, we cannot go back in time and change the past, although many of us have wanted to. However, we can absolutely change the future by courageously moving forward.

I believed that if I thought about a situation long enough I could finally find an answer to the plaguing question, "Why me?" What I discovered left me feeling even emptier. The people who create traumatic events are only thinking about one person, themselves. There is little or no solace or healing to be found in that answer.

Unable to find peace looking in that direction, the next logical solution was to pretend like it never happened—forget it. That didn't work either, because it did happen and nothing on this planet was going to change history.

I was so relieved to discover there was another option. Let us choose to engrave our traumatic life experiences on our heart and use them as reference points to better understand what others are experiencing. In doing so, there is finally, and I mean finally, purpose in our suffering, joy in our journey as walls come down and cooperation floods out, and ultimately, much needed healing in our soul.

We can change history by moving forward and positively impacting one future generation at a time. One day they will look back and thank us for our courage. We will have paid the price and broken the chains that bind with our unselfish gift of love.

Secrets

Can I relive the errors of yesterday and right them? Can I call back yesterday's wounds and make them whole? Can I become younger than yesterday? Can I take back the evil that was spoken, the blows that were struck, the pain that was caused? No. Yesterday is buried forever and I will think of it no more.

— Og Mandino

THERE IS ONE MORE contributor to low self-esteem— secrets. These are challenges that most often require professional intervention or treatment. They do not apply as broadly as the other challenges to self-esteem. If you are not struggling with any of these challenges, please feel free to move on to the next chapter.

Before we commence this part of our conversation, I must clearly state again that I am not a therapist. I am a coach. What I share comes from my personal experiences and observation. In no way will I attempt to give advice other than to emphasize the value in seeking assistance from a qualified therapist when you or a loved one is struggling.

At first blush, it would be easy to define *secrets* as significant inconsistencies between our public image and our private behavior—challenges that would be embarrassing if made public. We all have weaknesses. We all have areas in our lives that can be improved. Most have over-compensating behaviors of one kind or another. I do. This is different.

Common challenges that could lead to secret keeping include alcoholism, drug addiction, eating disorders, and neurobiological conditions such as depression. Significant differences between publically professed religious or political beliefs versus current secret and harmful behaviors can also have the same effect.

These struggles can create behaviors, usually experienced in private settings, for which there can be embarrassment and the suffering of physical and emotional pain by self or others. These feelings are often compounded by private feelings of shame.

Many of these challenges have their roots in very real medical conditions that cannot be *fixed* with a pill or a single therapy session. And because there are no visual external wounds to justify the obvious and often negative and harmful behaviors, we can be left disillusioned, confused and feeling hopeless. This malaise applies to both the one struggling with the challenge and those around them suffering from these consequences.

As a victim of someone's aberrant behavior, it is easy for us to say to the person struggling with depression, "Snap out of it. Just get over it." To the person struggling with substance abuse—alcohol and other forms of drugs—we might want to say, "Have some self control and just stop it." To the person struggling with a serious eating disorder, we might be tempted to say, "You look like skin and bones. You must be starving. For heaven sake, eat something, girl." To the person struggling with an addiction to pornography, we might want to say, "It's simple. Just press the delete button." To someone struggling with a sex addiction, we might want to say, "Just find a good companion and settle down like I did. You'll be so happy."

My greatest concern after traveling on this road with family members and many dear friends who are struggling, is that they can very easily reach a point of such desperation that terminal options might be considered. I often reflect on Og's story and how a single decision dramatically changed the course of his life forever.

It was a cold winter day in Cleveland, Ohio. The year was 1955. Burdened by the loss of his first wife and daughter due to his alcoholism, Og spent several years traveling the country in his old Ford, "*doing any kind of odd jobs in order to earn enough for another cheap bottle of wine.*" He spent countless drunken nights in the gutters, "*a sorry wretch of a human being, in a living hell.*"

One morning, as he walked by a pawnshop, he paused for a moment and looked in the display window. He saw a small handgun with a yellow price tag reading $29. He reached into his pocket and removed three ten-dollar bills, all that he had in the world.

He thought:

There's the end to all my problems. I'll buy the gun, get a couple of bullets, and take them back to that dingy room where I'm staying. Then I'll put the bullets in the gun, put the gun to my head, and pull the trigger, and I'll never have to face that miserable failure in the mirror ever again.

The snow began to fall. It was cold and windy. For some reason—one Og didn't even know at the time—he turned away from the window and began to walk. He made a different decision.

He didn't stop walking until he reached the public library. There he wandered among the thousands of books, searching for answers to his plaguing questions:

Where had I gone wrong? Could I make it with just a high school education? Was there any hope for me? What about my drinking problem? Was it too late for me? Was I doomed now to a life of frustration, failure, and fears?

That morning, Og commenced his ten-year journey of discovery and recovery. In time, his drinking subsided; he met and married Bette; he had two beautiful sons, and became the editor of *Success Magazine*. Today, he is known as one of the most prolific and beloved authors in history. Over fifty million copies of his books have been purchased. His impact on people's lives is far and wide—all starting with a single decision.

One of my clients, who was referred to a wonderful therapist, has been struggling with depression for some time. Over the past year several of her depressive episodes had been obvious and painful to those closest to her, but her most recent cycle of struggle was disguised even from them with a weak smile and reassurances that she "was just tired." This time it was the shame of relapse that drew her deeper inward until the pain could not be contained and flooded out.

Wanting to understand how to fix this hurting, her husband asked to attend one of her therapy sessions. To his credit, her husband is a tender, caring man, yet even he was surprised to discover the complexities and physical effects of depression on the brain. "This is caused by a very real medical challenge, you can't just make one change and fix it. It's not just a bad mood," he said with deeper understanding.

This beautiful mother of five, and consequently her family, is facing what will most likely be a life-long battle and their commitment together to be open about the subject and united in an effort to face it brings light to the darkness and dispels the secret.

Og writes:

There will be days when I must constantly struggle against forces that would tear me down.

Let's just make sure we are not struggling alone. Let's decide to get the professional assistance needed to adequately address these challenges. Let's embrace our uniqueness and intrinsic value and no longer feel less than or damaged. We are neither. We may simply be facing something that takes more than sheer determination. We would never expect a broken leg to heal by simply taking an x-ray.

Let us shed the shroud of secrecy and with it shame. There is healing in reaching out to others and in both giving and receiving support. The loneliness and hopelessness can be replaced with support and strength.

It may be true that due to our behavior when struggling with our challenge, we may have caused harm to others, but know that even this can be healed with time.

Very recently, I was a witness to the tender and merciful healing of a relationship between a father and his alcoholic son. For over forty years very real pain and resultant resentments have cankered both of their souls. With professional help, time, and amends, peace has finally again been restored. For this father, in the last years of his life suffering from serious heart problems, no greater gift of healing could have been given.

Og writes:

Why have I been allowed to live this extra day when others, far better than I, have departed? Is it that they have accomplished their purpose while mine is yet to be achieved? Is this another opportunity for me to become the man I know I can be? Is there a purpose in nature? Is this my day to excel? I will live this day as if it is my last.

I have seen and felt the miracles. It is time for yours to begin and with it the healing of your self-esteem. Today is your day. Take the next step and seek assistance from a qualified professional. You, and everyone you love, deserve this brave decision to move over and sit in the Observer's Chair.

Highest Level of Maturity

I am not on this earth by chance. I am here for a purpose and that purpose is to grow into a mountain, not to shrink to a grain of sand. Henceforth will I apply all my efforts to become the highest mountain of all and I will strain my potential until it cries for mercy.

— Og Mandino

THE OBJECTIVE—the target at which we take aim—is to *be* real, genuine and authentic, without the need to impress, pretend, feel shame or fear. Dr. Hartman called this "the most difficult task in our mortal existence." He concluded with this profound statement, "and the highest level of maturity."

I had always viewed maturity as an event that comes with age—not so. Maturity is measured by our desire to sit in the Observer's Chair, firmly planted, aware of any unhealthy habits of thinking, ready and willing to take whatever actions are needed to root these bad habits out of our lives.

Real, Genuine, and Authentic

Being real is all about creating relationships—mastering the art of connection. We love people. We are a good listener—we are safe. We ask empathetic questions—we create a safe place. People feel safe around us so the walls of resistance come down. We connect. Cooperation floods out and we are the beneficiaries.

Being genuine is all about owning our natural genius and bringing these gifts to the creation process and the service of others. We do not flaunt or brag about our gifts—we would only do that if we moved to the other chair. We do not cower or minimize our gifts or accomplishments—this would be another symptom of an over compensating victim stuck in *that* chair over there.

Loosed from restrictive and confining unhealthy habits of thinking, we set our genius free and focus on creating the most we can with the gifts that have been given. In doing so, we honor both our gifts and the Giver of these gifts.

Instead of engaging in constant daily dialogue with our unhealthy habits of thinking, we turn the Observer's Chair around, face the other direction, and carry on an elevated conversation with the Power of Creation. This is a good conversation. In response, inspired ideas, impressions, and solutions to challenges are manifest. Part of the brain that is normally dormant ignites. Passion is stirred. Action is the natural outcome.

Being authentic is about being our true self. We embrace

our *intrinsic goodness,* free from resistance, resentment, and rebellion. In this chair, we are self-directed—acting on our own moral authority, doing the next right thing for the right reason because *we* want to, get to, and choose to. We consciously make this choice.

The twin bulldozers of fear and obligation no longer have power to push us around. The unrelenting, unyielding bully of the unachievable—perfection—no longer demeans the quality of our efforts. We sit in our chair, gripping the armrests, self-determined, disciplined, and focused on excellence.

Impress

In a vain attempt to secure attention, admiration, or respect from others and due to a lack of self-esteem, our unhealthy habits may want us to impress people by emphasizing the magnitude of our possessions, contributions, or the importance of our ideas and opinions.

When we let these habits determine our value based on how well we perform, how much money we make or the things we own, we can find our self in a deep, dense, black hole that can never be filled. We remain bound in the chair of our unhealthy habits.

A few years ago I had a funny yet poignant experience that I hesitate to share, but here goes.

You may remember the ridiculous story about my Rolex watch that I told in my first book, *Today I Begin a New Life,* and how I wore it like a watch model? Then there were the Mercedes, the Ferrari, and the Porsches. I was my house, my cars, my stuff—this is where I got my self-worth. Of course, by the grace of God, they were taken away so that I could learn some valuable lessons about that which is most important.

A few years later after things turned around financially, I bought another sports car. It was Harrison Ford's Jet Black Acura NSX. It was fast and fun—like a road-hugging go-cart on steroids. Unlike the Ferrari, it was dependable—at least that's how I justified buying it at the time. I kept it for a few years, sold it, and bought a newer NSX. The second was a red T-top with a tan interior.

One day while driving to the office with the top off, it hit me, "You are becoming your stuff again."

"No," I exclaimed. "Make it not so."

We had purchased two old historic houses in downtown Salt Lake City and renovated them. Our office was in one, and we rented the second. In the back of the property there was a warehouse and an old dilapidated single-car garage.

When I got to the office, I put the NSX in the garage, and covered it. "You will stay here until I'm certain I am *not* my stuff," I lovingly said as I left and locked the garage—and no, the car did not speak back, thankfully. This action may seem extreme, but retrospectively, it served.

The car hibernated in the garage for nine months. During that time, I drove an older model Honda Civic with a crack in the windshield.

One day I decided it was time to move forward. I unlocked the garage, took the cover off the car, and climbed in. Of course, the battery was dead, but so was my unhealthy attachment. I jumped the battery, and off I went, back into life with renewed perspective. Two months later we sold the car and bought two Hondas.

We do not need to be a self-denying martyr to learn this wisdom. We need not park our lives in a garage for nine months to figure this out. Owning nice things is great. We just don't want these things to be the basis of our self-worth.

When we see this kind of bravado from others, which is a common over compensation for a lack of self-esteem, let us not be offended or disgusted. Let us instead silently and to our self say, "I love you. You are beyond price." Let's give 'em a hug if we can—they need one.

Consider: Am I attached to any *thing*? Is my identity tied to my house, car, career, accumulated wealth, etc.? If all of this were taken away tomorrow, what would be left of me? If I was attached to my things and have lost these things, can I let go now and be okay? What would be different if I didn't need stuff to feel better about my self?

When we find our self tied down to *that* chair over there by the tether of impress, cut it loose, stand up, and get back in the Observer's Chair as quickly as we can.

Pretend

Ramona and I attended a lecture in 1992. To make his point, the speaker asked us to stand and wander around the room, mingling and greeting one another. Suddenly he said, "Stop!" He then instructed us to face the person closest to us.

"I want you to tell this person your deepest darkest secret," he said.

You have to be kidding, I thought. I was very uncomfortable and wanted to leave immediately, but decided to play along—and I am so glad I did.

The man standing closest to me was about 5' 11" tall, weighed about 130 lbs dripping wet, had long, stringy hair and an ashen, pocked complexion. I let him go first. He bowed his head and shared with some reservation, "I am a drug addict."

I wanted to say, "Yes, okay, but what's your *secret*?" It didn't take long to get the point of the exercise.

Most of the time when we're sitting over there in *that* chair and our thoughts want us to pretend that we are something other than we are, we may think we're fooling everyone, but the only person we're fooling is our self. We seem to be the last to know what everyone else already knows. When we try to fool others, it can be dangerous; when we try to fool our self, it can be debilitating.

For a moment, let's consider the current state of the economy. Are we hanging onto anything we can no longer afford to own? Are we pretending about the true condition of our finances? This examination can be poignant. It was for me.

Interestingly, 92% of those actively seeking abundance have an unhealthy thought process that is over-focused on the outward appearances of others—possessions, accomplishments, contributions, performance, talents, skills.

When this thought process wants us to put too much value on outward appearances, and it *looks* like everyone else is okay, we may believe what we see. Even worse, we may compare these superficial and inaccurate impressions against our internal dialogue about our self. The result is a cruel game of comparison and we lose.

When we look around, what do we see? Does everyone look okay—financially secure, with ideal relationships, and perfect lives? In these moments, have we ever felt alone, tarnished, damaged, or less than? Wanting to fit in, did we perpetuate this illusion by pretending we were okay?

Herein lies the real danger. If we are struggling financially and others *look* like they aren't having any challenges, we may believe that we're the only one suffering. We may feel a need to pretend that everything is okay with us, too. We may spend money we don't have and borrow money we cannot afford to pay back.

As it turned out, the perpetuation of this lie *that everyone appears to be okay except me, and I must pretend in order to belong,* was one of the major contributors to the recession of 2008. In the end, the thick façade of our fragile credit-driven economy surrendered to the realities of our life circumstances and real cash flows.

A few years later, foreclosures continue to abound. Credit-card defaults continue to soar. Lives and families continue to be torn apart. Even nations reel from the burden of debt.

The wounds are deep because of the vast disparity between outward appearances and the bedrock of reality on which we can build a true recovery. The fallout has threatened to shake the very foundation of our personal lives and the world's financial system.

Over the decade prior to 2008, pretending was in fashion. The unbridled spending that was needed to create the appearance of wealth enjoyed unprecedented popularity. It was as if we thought we could spend our way into prosperity. All the while the Observer's Chair sat vacant. In the history books, this time will be looked upon with infamy. Few have escaped, and the damage to self-esteem is nearly incalculable.

The answer is not to carry our challenges and woes on our sleeve for all to see. The invitation is to shift from pretending to being real, genuine, and authentic. This requires that we again occupy the Observer's Chair. This shift in our energy and intention is both discernable and inviting.

Our debts may not be paid yet or even soon, but we are finally focusing on what matters most. Healing can begin.

Shame

I remember a scene from one of my favorite movies, *The Mission*. The character played by Robert DeNiro is a mercenary and slave trader who has killed many people, including his own brother.

Seeking penance, he fills to overflowing a large net with all of his weapons of war. He then drags this heavy, bulky burden behind him for miles. He forges a raging river, struggles up a steep mud-covered mountainside and then scales a treacherous cliff adjacent the Iguazu Falls. His destination is a secluded, primitive area inhabited only by the indigenous peoples he had previously hunted.

Arriving at the top, he is quickly surrounded by natives. One native draws a knife and approaches. Just as we think the native is going to exact revenge by cutting his throat, he instead cuts the rope, freeing the repentant man of his burden. He wept.

Many of us know this sack, the steep climb, the grace that frees, and the tears that flow—the singular gift that can heal deep wounds.

The word *shame* comes from the root word *sham*, which means "to make a covering (like a pillow sham)." When we feel guilt, we feel bad about what we have done. Shame is a much deeper, piercing feeling—we feel bad about who we are. When we feel shame, our natural genius is covered by a heavy blanket of self-deprecating thought processes that suffocate both our goodness and gifts.

Can we see our self over there in *that* chair with a heavy, cold, wet blanket covering us—every once in a while peeking out wondering if anyone knows what we have done. How often do we reflect on a past mistake and ask, "How could I have ever done that?" or, "How can I ever be worthy?" or, "What have I lost out on because of what I've done?" or, "They will never forgive me."

We have all made mistakes—missed the mark, fallen short. Let us take off the blanket of shame and take the short walk over here to the Observer's Chair. Here we can find grace and healing.

It's time to ask a different question: "In what ways have all of these experiences uniquely prepared me to serve others?" Ask this and our experiences can finally serve a worthy purpose.

Fear

The fourth and final tether is *fear*. When I was in the sixth grade, one of my responsibilities was washing the family car in preparation for Sunday. At the time we lived in Woodbine, Georgia. Our home sat on the street that divided the wet swamp from the dry swamp. When the seasons changed, we had an occasional encounter with a wild animal or reptile. This was one of those days.

I had gone in the house to get a glass of water. As I walked out the back door and began to descend the steps to the carport, a large timber rattler confronted me. It immediately coiled and its rattles started blazing. It was not happy.

I froze and called out to my dad. He came running. Dad reached for a shovel, and in one fell swoop, cut off the rattler's head. When I posed for pictures with the snake, the rattler stretched 5' 2", was three inches in diameter, and had ten rattles and an eleventh forming on the end, called a button. To this day, the sound of a rattlesnake in action sends chills down my spine.

This kind of fear is created by a real or present danger, such as a deadly reptile or an abusive person. However, another kind of fear can be equally paralyzing, and the source of this fear is our unhealthy habits of thinking.

When we engage in destructive thought processes such as fantasy or fatigue-driven pessimism, the body releases molecules that leave us feeling anxious, stressed, and frustrated. Impaired, our intuition misreads these emotional signals as a real threat. After all, it *feels* like one. Subsequently, our mind releases additional, and even more chronic doses of cortisol. Thus, as stated by an unknown author, fear is nothing more than False Evidence Appearing Real.

Og writes:

Can I perform tomorrow's deeds while standing in today's path? Can I place tomorrow's gold in today's purse? Should I concern myself over events which I may never witness? Should I torment myself with problems that may never come to pass? No! Tomorrow lies buried with yesterday, and I will think of it no more. I will live this day as if it is my last.

Summary

The need to impress, pretend, feel shame, and fear can keep us tied down in the chair of our bad habits. These four tethers can rob us, and everyone around us, of our natural genius and intrinsic goodness.

Each tether is a cord that binds—each tether is self-focused. When we surrender to these unhealthy habits of thinking, we may create money, but we'll never be truly wealthy. We may be in a relationship, but never in a partnership. We may look good, but never *feel* good about our self.

To be real, genuine, and authentic, we want to sit firmly planted in the Observer's Chair. To do this, we want to let go of the need to impress, pretend, feel shame, and fear. The most important of all is to let go of fear.

Raising Awareness

Today I begin a new life. Today I shed my old skin which hath too long suffered the bruises of failure and the wounds of mediocrity. Today I am born anew and my birthplace is a vineyard where there is fruit for all.

— Og Mandino

EACH TIME we are aware and consciously make the decision to sit in the Observer's Chair, we are beginning our new life. We are shedding our old skin. Whether we find the need to make this decision daily or even hourly, the impact on our happiness and peace of mind hangs in the balance.

Look over at the chair of our unhealthy habits of thinking. Imagine sitting in *that* chair while the baseball bat of life mercilessly takes its swings destroying our self-esteem. Can we see it? Can we feel it? After all, if I said half the things to you that your unhealthy habits of thinking say to you, could we still be friends?

When we stand, and move back over here to the Observer's Chair, we shed our bruised and wounded skin, and leave it over there. We become our real and true self. And each time we make this decision, we are born anew.

This birthplace is a vineyard and there is fruit for all because we are no longer trapped in our unhealthy habits of thinking. Instead of focusing on taking, getting, receiving—being fed, we are finally free—whole and complete—ready to focus on feeding others.

This kind of healing can occur only when we choose to sit in our chair—the Observer's Chair and we will want to know how to get in this chair sooner and stay here longer.

Hearing for the First Time

I clearly remember when I heard it for the first time—consciously heard it. I was an adult. I was standing in the bathroom looking in the mirror reflecting on a recent decision. Let's just say, things didn't turn out the way I had planned.

Coming from somewhere deep down inside the dark recesses of my mind, like puss from a festering wound, toxic dialogue spewed out, "David, you are *so* stupid!"

Though consciously hearing these words for the first time, sadly they were not unfamiliar. It was crystal clear in that moment—my unhealthy habits of thinking had been reciting this sentiment for decades. The reverberating echo was deafening.

I pondered, *How often have I allowed these words to be*

uttered? What kind of damage has been caused? In what ways has this unconscious and repeated comment imprisoned my future? The answers revealed many a lost opportunity.

Now aware, I made the conscious decision to stand, walk over, and sit in the Observer's Chair. From this vantage point I could make new and better choices. The desire and willingness to be aware and hear has led to several more moments of discovery—powerful pivotal moments of personal growth.

It is time to learn how to be conscious and alert—aware—so that when unhealthy habits of thinking come calling, we are not unknowingly enticed to follow. Here are some great tools to raise and maintain awareness.

Intentional Creation Assessment

Awareness begins with measurement. Which thoughts support us in sitting in the Observer's Chair? Which thoughts are occasionally, frequently or even consistently attempting to sabotage our efforts to stay here? Now we can know with laser accuracy using the Intentional Creation Assessment.

This FREE Assessment introduces us to all Six Qualities of an Intentional Creator:

- Self-Esteem
- Connection with People
- Mental Creation
- Physical Creation

- Discipline and Structure
- Joy in the Journey

Each Quality is in turn divided into Six Foundational Characteristics. The Characteristics for Self-Esteem are as follows:

- Whole and Complete
- Confident
- Valiant
- Peaceful
- Deliberate
- Unconditional

The Assessment measures the underlying thought processes for each Characteristic helping us to know where to focus our time and attention in order to maximize results.

When you are ready, go to the Appendix and discover how you can take a FREE Intentional Creation Assessment.

The Ten Scrolls

Neuroscientists tell us that to facilitate real and lasting changes in our unhealthy habits of thinking, we want a tool that creates density focus—consistent, conscious awareness. We plan in days, weeks, months and years, but we live in pivotal moments of decision. We want tools that help keep our awareness heightened throughout the day. Og Mandino's Ten

Scrolls are one of these tools.

When Og was writing the bestselling book, *The Greatest Salesman in the World*, he wanted the centerpiece to be what he called, "The ten time-tested principles of success." The beginning and ending of the book had been completed, but Og was experiencing a severe case of writer's block.

He had set up the ten principles as the "wisdom from the ages" passed down for thousands of years from generation to generation. What should they say? With the book deadline approaching fast, Og was feeling increasingly inadequate. Bette, Og's sweetheart, would later share with a wry smile, "He was getting a little ornery."

When I read one of the first drafts of this book to Ramona, she stopped me right here and with one of her famous grins, asked, "I wonder which chair Og was sitting in?" We both smiled but I knew she was also giving me a gentle reminder of which chair she likes me to sit in during moments of uncertainty. I digress.

Og took two days off from work as the editor of *Success Magazine*. On the evening of the second day, after tucking his two boys in bed, Og received an inspired idea that launched a fourteen-hour, all night long flood of inspiration—the Ten Scrolls were written.

Looking back over the past four plus decades, it is clear that the veracity of that inspired experience has passed the test of time. Twenty-five million people now own the book.

The story is charming—Hafid, the camel boy, wanting to find success—Pathros, his boss, giving him Ten Scrolls that contained the wisdom of the ages—Hafid using the principles in the Scrolls to become one of the wealthiest men in the region—but the real secret still rests in the power of the words in the Scrolls.

Inspired and intuitively written in the language of the intrinsic, the Scrolls come to the reader serving up unlimited interpretations and unlimited applications for almost any life circumstance. Each time we read a Scroll we learn a new and deeper lesson. After fifteen years I am still getting valuable insights.

Even more important than the lessons learned, as we read a Scroll morning, noon, and night, our awareness is heightened and remains more consistent throughout the day. Other than holy writ, for me, and thousands and thousands of others, the Ten Scrolls are one of the best tools for creating density focus so we are better prepared to respond favorably when faced with one of those pivotal moments of decision.

Go to Appendix: Resources, and discover how you can access Og's narration of the Ten Scrolls for FREE.

Affirmations

Being aware, we can more clearly hear when our unhealthy habits of thinking are spewing toxic dialogue. We can hear it for what it is. In these pivotal moments we can choose to stand and move back over to the Observer's Chair. Once we make the decision to move, what can help keep us here?

Below we find six powerful affirmations, one for each of the Six Characteristics of Self-Esteem. Each is intentionally stated as an "I am" affirmation—the voice of the Observer—our real voice. As we listen to these affirmations over and over, they serve as a constant reminder of the person we want to become.

I am whole and complete. I enjoy being me and am comfortable in my own skin. I recognize and embrace my irreplaceable value. I am fully available to serve others.

I am confident. I own my clay. I embrace my uniqueness and natural genius and act free of hesitation, doubt and fear.

I am valiant. I am true to my own beliefs and values. They are engraved on my heart, shape my character, and guide my actions.

I am peaceful. I am comfortable with my own ideas and opinions and allow others to have opposing ideas and opinions without the need to openly defend mine.

I am deliberate. I set appropriate boundaries regarding how I allocate my time and talents. I agree to do things for the right reason.

I am unconditional. I see my strengths and weaknesses in balance. Yesterday's misfortunes, yesterday's defeats, yesterday's aches of the heart are powerless. I stay present in the NOW and in creation.

These are not just good ideas. These affirmations come from a deep understanding of Axiological Mathematics—a formal science used in the Intentional Creation Assessment to measure how we think. When our thoughts are congruent with this math, they reveal the voice of the Observer—the person we want to become, our true self.

Becoming Affirmations

In the past, we may have attempted to use affirmations that focus more on *having* versus *becoming*. For example: "I am wealthy. I attract powerful people into my life. I have an estate home, a vacation home, several expensive vehicles and a monthly income of $50,000."

Having affirmations focus on getting, taking, and receiving. These secret desires and real intentions, which center primarily on the pursuit of ease and comfort, drive escape and avoid fantasy. This creates unrealistic expectations, that when unmet, foster disappointment, frustration and fear.

The natural outcome of *having* affirmations is self-loathing and ultimately the destruction of self-esteem. In short, and for the vast majority of the population, *having* affirmations do not support a person staying firmly planted in the Observer's Chair. Instead they keep us stuck—imprisoned in the chair of our unhealthy habits of thinking.

On the other hand, *becoming* affirmations focus on changing our character—the person we want to become. Our secret desires and real intentions are to engage in life, embrace principles, connect with and serve others, create value everywhere we go and with everyone we meet, and contribute to and enrich the world.

Foundationally, we cannot become an outcome. For example, we may have wealth but we are not wealth. However, we can become Whole and Complete, one of the Characteristics of Self-Esteem. When we do so, we feel a deep sense of personal worth. We experience peace of mind and the joy of being fully available to serve others. We are comfortable in our own skin.

"I am" *becoming* affirmations help us to get and stay grounded. Once here, they prepare us to learn and master the principles, practices and processes for becoming an Intentional Creator.

As we repeat these *becoming* affirmations over and over and over again, we will begin to develop a hunger for getting here sooner and staying here longer. There is a very good reason. Each time we make the decision to be here and focus on *becoming*, we immediately begin to experience joy.

Here is Og's promise should we choose to focus on becoming:

I will begin to awake, each morning, with a vitality I have never known before. My vigor will increase, my enthusiasm will rise, my desire to meet the world will overcome every fear I once knew at sunrise, and I will be happier than I ever believed it possible to be in this world of strife and sorrow.

Summary

Again, the tools we can use to raise our awareness are the measurements in the Intentional Creation Assessment, the Ten Scrolls, and the "I am" *becoming* affirmations provided.

When you are ready, go to the Appendix at the end of the book to get information about how you can take a FREE Intentional Creation Assessment, access the recording of the Ten Scrolls narrated by Og, and access the recording of the affirmations for Self-Esteem.

Creating New Habits

In truth, the only difference between those who have failed and those who have succeeded lies in the difference of their habits. Good habits are the key to all success. Bad habits are the unlocked door to failure. Thus, the first law I will obey, which preceedeth all others is — I will form good habits.

— Og Mandino

NEUROSCIENTISTS tell us that the brain has neuroplasticity—the ability to be shaped and molded—rewired. Yes, we can create new neuropathways—new habits of thinking.

Neuroscientists also tell us that when a new habit is formed—a new neuropathway—the brain synapically prunes off the old habit much like we prune a dead branch off of a tree. This is the key that unlocks the door to success—replacing bad habits with good habits.

Destroying the Monsters

No matter how our unhealthy habits of thinking were formed, we have the power to change them. We are not destined to flounder and fail. We have been created to succeed—we are the Observer. I find this reality nothing short of miraculous.

Og writes:

> *Failure no longer will be my payment for struggle. Just as nature made no provision for my body to tolerate pain neither has it made any provision for my life to suffer failure. Failure, like pain, is alien to my life. In the past I accepted it as I accepted pain. Now I reject it and I am prepared for wisdom and principles which will guide me out of the shadows into the sunlight of wealth, position, and happiness far beyond my most extravagant dreams until even the golden apples in the Garden of Hesperides will seem no more than my just reward.*

In mythology, the golden apples in the Garden of Hesperides were guarded by the hundred-headed dragon, Ladon. Hercules had to first "prune" off the multiple heads of this serpent. Once accomplished, the golden apples were his just reward—but prune the heads first, he must.

Our dragons are not mythological. They are very real. They are our unhealthy habits of thinking lying in wait over in *that* chair. Like Hercules, we too, will want to prune the heads off of these mental monsters.

Og writes:

*My bad habits must be destroyed and new furrows pre-
pared for good seed.*

New Furrows

Some of our mental monsters may be difficult to destroy,
but destroy them we must. We do so by preparing new furrows and planting good seeds—and may I say in reference to
Og's mythological and deeply metaphorical reference—golden
apple seeds.

Herein lies one of our greatest opportunities and also one of
our greatest challenges. The decision to change a habit of thinking is ours. It requires that we exercise our free will by repeat-
edly preparing new furrows and proactively planting new seeds.

Will it be easy? No. Will it at times seem Herculean?
Possibly. Can it be accomplished? Absolutely, yes! And when
these old habits are pruned off, what are the *fruits* of *our* labors?
The golden apples of success, happiness and peace of mind will
be no more than our just reward, the very things for which we
hunger.

The alternative is nearly unfathomable. Should we shrink
from this task because our monsters seem too fierce, we are left
with only one of two options. One, we surrender our free will
and spend our life nursing the inevitable bruises of failure and
the wounds of mediocrity. Or, two, we will need to find a way

to play life small enough to avoid awakening *our* monsters.

Can we all agree? Let's start preparing some new furrows.

Planting Good Seeds

To assist us, I have created some examples of unhealthy and even toxic internal dialogue. There are examples for each of the Six Characteristics of Self-Esteem. Each is followed by an "I am" *becoming* affirmation. Our objective is to hear when we are sitting in *that* chair over there—the toxic dialogue—and proactively choose to prepare new furrows to the Observer's Chair—the *becoming* affirmations.

Some of this dialogue may apply and some may not. However, when the dialogue sounds *all too familiar*, repeat the following words aloud, "That is not like me." Then read the accompanying "I am" *becoming* affirmation and say aloud, "This *is* me." This *is* who we really are—the person sitting in the Observer's Chair—taking the appropriate actions needed to become this Characteristic.

We may hear our monster shouting, "That's not true!" It may even provide us with examples—recent and ancient. Openly acknowledge your unhealthy habits by saying aloud, "Yes, when I surrender my free will to you, I do some pretty crazy things." Smile and conclude with the following, "Today I choose to be the Observer of my thoughts. Today I choose to sit in the Observer's Chair."

When we think this way, we are not pretending to be someone other than who we are, but rather practicing to be the person we want to become.

Always remember, we are not our thoughts, but these thoughts—these bad habits of thinking—these monsters—can wreak havoc in our life. Some habits may have a powerful grip on us right now. Let's read and listen and practice shifting. Underline the phrases that sound the most familiar or add some of your own:

Whole and Complete: What is wrong with me? I can almost touch it. I can almost taste it. Why can't I have it? Does God not love me? What's the use? I'm so stupid. I knew better. Why did that happen to me? I should have stopped it. I never get the answers I need. I never make the money I need. Who do I think I am, anyway? I will never be allowed to do that.

Add a few of your own: _____

"That is not like me!"

Affirmation: I am whole and complete. I enjoy being me and am comfortable in my own skin. I recognize and embrace my irreplaceable value. I am fully available to serve others.

"This *is* me!"

Confident: I wish I had her hair (body, personality, charisma, skill, intelligence, education). I wish I had his car (home, bank account, financial freedom). I am so ugly (fat, old, bald, short, tall, slow). I should have married someone else (had more children, less children, more successful children, raised my children differently, listened more, showed up more, been more loving). I am such a failure compared to the rest of my friends (family, co-workers, community, church members). I should have had a different career (invested more wisely, spent or borrowed less money, sold sooner, stayed in longer, had a different business partner). I don't have the time or energy to start over again. I don't know how long I can keep doing this. Why did I do that? What's the use in even trying?

Add a few of your own: _____

"That is not like me!"

Affirmation: I am confident. I own my clay. I embrace my uniqueness and natural genius and act free of hesitation, doubt and fear.

"This *is* me!"

Valiant: I'm not sure anymore what is right or wrong. Maybe it was a bad idea. I am uncomfortable doing that but I want to get the promotion (make the money, fit it, be accepted, keep the peace). Why did I say that? I should have kept my mouth shut. I couldn't help myself. I feel so strongly about it! Frankly, I don't care if I am obnoxious. It has to be done this way. It's the rule (regulation, policy procedure, gospel, needed quality).

Add a few of your own: _____

"That is not like me!"

Affirmation: I am valiant. I am true to my own beliefs and values. They are engraved on my heart, shape my character, and guide my actions.

"This *is* me!"

Peaceful: I am right. Who do they think they are? I have studied this for years. Do they not respect me? I don't like confrontation. I just want to maintain the peace even if I have to sacrifice me. Why can't we all just get along?

Add a few of your own: _____

"That is not like me!"

Affirmation: I am peaceful. I am comfortable with my own ideas and opinions and allow others to have opposing ideas and opinions without the need to openly defend mine.

"This *is* me!"

Deliberate: I have to, I should, I must do it. Who will do it if I don't? What will they think of me if I say, "No?" I know

I'm swamped but I'm better at doing this than anyone else. It has to be done right. I feel so depleted (empty, exhausted, numb).

Add a few of your own: _____

"That is not like me!"

Affirmation: I am deliberate. I set appropriate boundaries regarding how I allocate my time and talents. I agree to do things for the right reason.

"This *is* me!"

Unconditional: I am such a failure. There is no use in even trying. It's too late. I can never make up for that. I have violated the laws of heaven and earth. There is no forgiveness for me. Maybe I should just end it all.

Add a few of your own: _____

"That is not like me!"

Affirmation: I am unconditional. I recognize my strengths and weaknesses in balance. I stay present in the now and resist the temptation to waste valuable time mourning yesterday's misfortunes, yesterday's defeats, yesterday's aches of the heart.

"This *is* me!"

As we become increasingly aware of our unhealthy habits, especially when they are the dominant voice in our mind—the biggest monsters—we can step back and ask, "Is this what I really want? Does this dialogue serve me in preparing new furrows and planting good seeds and growing the golden apples of success, happiness and peace of mind?" Not surprisingly, the answer is always, "No!"

Nurturing the Seeds

Let us repeat this process over and over again. Every time we encounter one of our monsters, let us choose to sit in the Observer's Chair. Let's take the action to maintain higher levels of awareness so that each time one of these pivotal moments of decision arises, we can consciously make this new and better choice.

With these new furrows constantly being prepared, good seeds always being planted, and with proper nourishment, we can grow new habits. And it's time to break out the pruning sheers.

It may also be important to note: When we are unconscious of our thoughts, and then choose to become conscious, it is not unusual to discover that our thoughts are less than positive and supportive. Please know, whatever we discover, awareness does not create monsters, but instead reveals them.

We will also want to be grateful for any life experiences, personal or business, challenging or joyful, which help raise our awareness and help reveal our monsters. Now we know what to do. Now we can begin to grow new habits.

Summary

As uncomfortable as it may be to sit in *that* chair over there, it may be all that we have known until now. At first, our fear of the unknown—what is possible—may be greater than our fear of the known—our monsters. Thus we can begin to understand why the pain is not in change, but is in the resistance to change.

Take courage. Stand and move over and occupy the Observer's Chair—you are the rightful owner. You will know, the moment you make the decision to move, that it was a good one. You will feel it. There is an intrinsic knowing when we are in this chair. This is an amazing place to live.

James Allen writes:

Let a man radically alter his thoughts, and he will be astonished at the rapid transformation it will effect in the material conditions of his life.

Lastly, until a new habit is fully-grown—reaching full maturity—we want to be hyper vigilant. Young habits that are still in their infancy are very fragile. All we have to do is drop them and they break. As one client recently said, "If I miss a morning and afternoon of reading the Scrolls, by night I find myself right back in the chair of my unhealthy habits of thinking."

Action

Only action determines my value in the market place and to multiply my value I will multiply my actions. I will walk where the failure fears to walk. I will work when the failure seeks rest. I will talk when the failure remains silent. I will call on ten who can buy my goods while the failure makes grand plans to call on one. I will say it is done before the failure says it is too late. I will act now.

— OG MANDINO

WHEN WE break creation down into its smallest and most important common denominator, we finally arrive at a pivotal moment, that moment in time when we reach out and touch the NOW—the timeline of our life.

Pivotal Moments

Pivotal moments represent the millimeters of creation. This is where physical creation takes place. This is where success is created. This is where joy is experienced. This is where we meet our natural genius. This is where we meet our true self. This is all about sitting in the Observer's Chair.

As mentioned earlier, we plan our life in days, weeks, months, and years. We live our lives in pivotal moments. It's in these pivotal moments that we face decisions. The choices we make in these pivotal moments determine success or failure. After all, success is nothing more than a series of wisely executed pivotal moments.

Ultimately, while living in the NOW and taking action, we are aware and focus our energy on the millimeters of creation. We no longer waste our day escaping into the future to a time when we will be rich, when success will be ours. We know that if we engage in fantasy we waste valuable and critical pivotal moments attempting to prematurely experience something we have not yet earned—and most likely will never have if we continue to follow this pattern of thinking. Our expectations will remain unmet and our potential untapped—and our self-esteem compromised.

Passion-Driven Action

When we bring our passion into the now there is a deep desire to create in tangible reality that which was so clearly manifest in our mind. We work passion-driven and are endowed with even more ability. People are put on our path who can serve us and whom we can serve.

Conscious and passion-driven, we step back, take control of our thought processes, exercise our agency, choose to be self-directed and choose to make wise decisions. In doing so we consciously shift the outcome from confusion to "Yes, I did that!" In these moments we receive the prize that comes only at the end of each pivotal moment, the joy of accomplishment and it is empowering. It is also healing.

For example, we commit to a daily exercise program. Today is cardio, thirty minutes on the treadmill. We have been putting it off and avoiding it all day. "Anything, give me anything to do except that!" Then in a conscious pivotal moment we reflect on our vision of a healthy body. We see it clearly in our mind and the very idea ignites our passion.

We face the moment and finally hear the unhealthy habits of thinking that have been sabotaging our decision to exercise— "I have so much to do!" "I am too tired!" "I will do that later! Really I will!"—all first person, all counterfeit voices coming from *that* chair over there.

I—the real me—the Observer—I consciously take control and choose differently. I put on my running shoes and mount the treadmill. There is a new sense of purpose. I act on my own moral authority. No one is forcing me. Alive, in control and connected to my soul, I choose to push even harder than in past sessions. I feel empowered. When the thirty minutes is up I am energized and hopeful.

Over time, we wisely execute a series of these pivotal

moments regarding exercise and we reach our goal whatever it may be—a certain weight, a certain distance, a specific state of health. We experience success. It did not just happen, it was intentionally created in the pivotal moments of living and we independently made the decision to sit in the Observer's Chair and *do* it.

Food for the Soul

Sitting here, we choose to read the Scrolls as prescribed by Og in Scroll I. As we read a Scroll three times a day for thirty days, we come prepared, ready to be fed. We more easily overcome thought processes that resist and rebel. We come to increase our awareness with a desire to be prepared for whatever comes our way that day.

We know the Scrolls were written in the language of the intrinsic—metaphor and poetry—and provide us with unlimited interpretations and unlimited applications. When our heart is open, the Scrolls come to us. They feed our soul.

Small Acts Repeated

We discover that all of these pivotal moments throughout the day are as Og calls them, the childish swipes of an ax that eventually cause the large oak to fall, the raindrops that wash away a mountain, the ant that devours the tiger, the stars that fill the sky, the bricks from which we build our castle.

There are many positive forces at play in creation, but in the end, we make our choices in these pivotal moments. We know that no one else can make those choices for us.

Og writes:

"I know that small attempts, repeated, will complete any undertaking . . . I will command and I will obey my own command."

We discover that action is the result of a wise decision made in a pivotal moment—by our true self.

Summary

When Og said that to increase our value we must increase our actions, we may think that he was only talking about the value others place on us. Og was also talking about the value we place on our self. When in passion-driven action we have not only touched the NOW on the timeline of our life, we have just met our true self—"I am." I am the one who chooses wisely. We become whole and complete by doing the next right thing for the right reason.

Stillness

Never will I allow my mind to be attracted to evil and despair, rather I will uplift it with the knowledge and wisdom of the ages. Never will I allow my soul to become complacent and satisfied, rather I will feed it with meditation and prayer. Never will I allow my heart to become small and bitter, rather I will share it and it will grow and warm the earth.

— Og Mandino

WE ARE NOT OUR THOUGHTS. We are the Observer of these thoughts. As we practice the process of quieting our mind so we can step back, listen, and observe, it becomes easier and easier to distinguish between the real YOU and your thoughts. Some of these thoughts do not want us to step back. They want us to believe this is who we are. Nothing is further from the truth.

I would like to do a little exercise to assist all of us in quieting our mind. It is important that you are in a quiet place.

Are you ready?

(Read the following or log on: <u>www.ogmandinogroup.com/</u> <u>audio</u> and listen)

Take a seat in the Observer's Chair. Settle in and get comfortable. Close your eyes and relax your head—your neck—your shoulders. Good.

From here, look over at *that* chair over there and notice your unhealthy habits of thinking. Can you see them?

These old habits were born somewhere along life's journey. Perhaps one came from a parent; another from a childhood experience; another from a lost love; another from a companion. There is a story behind each one of them, isn't there?

Notice how several of them are masquerading as ghoulish monsters. Some are growling, others clawing the air—all trying to act tough and intimidating. Can you see them? Smile at each of them and wave.

In truth they are fragile and have depended on you for their support, and support them we have (smile).

Let all of your unhealthy habits of thinking go. You are no longer deceived by the clothes they wear.

Let go of the one that questions your worth or worthiness—the ugliest one. Let go of the one that wants you to compare your self with others—the most ungrateful one.

Let go of doubt and fear—the meanest ones. Let go of the ones called ease and comfort—the deadliest ones. They make you feel euphoric for a little while and then clobber you with the club of reality. Lots of bruises from these crazy thoughts—criminal. Look, it's still trying to sell you that easy button.

Let go of the one called Busy, Busy, Busy—the most exhausting one. It's the one over there running around like a chicken with its head cut off. That one has nearly worn you ragged.

Let go of the one that wants you to impress others or wants you to pretend things are better than they are. Let go of the one that wants you to feel shame about a weakness or imperfection and the one that wants you to act strong, smart, or perfect. Let them all go.

Usually this is the time when one of your thoughts gets very active and frankly a bit nervous. From one you may hear advice about how dumb or silly this activity may seem. Another thought may try to convince YOU that this is nonsense and YOU can't live without them.

Another may advise you to act frustrated, tired, disinterested, or pre-occupied.

Another may argue that there is something inherently wrong with letting your mind "be quiet" so YOU can experience YOU. The most insecure thoughts may advise YOU that YOU are giving up control of your life when in fact you are finally taking control of your thoughts.

Acknowledge your thoughts. Thank them for their input, and then let them go. Remember, YOU are not your thoughts. YOU are the Observer.

You are finally free to be the real you, the Observer of your thoughts. Welcome home.

Take a few slow, deep breaths. Notice the air filling your lungs and then being expelled. Notice the stillness and the peace in your mind.

Take a few more slow, deep breaths and let it all in. Let in the inspired whispers, the visions of possibility coming from a Higher Source. Let them ignite your passion and drive your actions. Can you hear it? Can you see it in your mind's eye?

This is the conversation YOU will want to engage in. Feel the peace that comes from here versus the confusion, frustration, and fear that exist over there in *that* other chair.

If your thoughts are still trying to get your attention, know that they are very uncomfortable with the idea that YOU can carry on a conversation with another Source, while excluding them. Just relax. You are sitting safely in the Observer's Chair.

How often have YOU allowed your thoughts to control YOU? Do they want you to come home to their little den of destruction? If they are talking, notice what they're saying, don't judge them, just notice them and let them go. Exhale.

Take a few more slow deep breaths and continue to relax and observe. Quiet your unhealthy thoughts when they jump back into action. Notice them and then let them go. There is nothing to do, nothing to try, nothing to get right, just be at peace, and Observe.

From here the need to impress others seems shallow; the need to pretend, immature; the need to feel shame, wasteful; and the need to fear, childish. Here you know who you are. Here you sit in your gifts connected with the real Source of Inspiration.

Notice your body, your fingers, your toes, your eyes, and your nose. Don't make any judgments, just continue to relax, and observe. Each time you find this place, YOU know that YOU are not dependent on any mortal or any material thing to be whole and complete.

From here YOU can simply be YOU, real and genuine and authentic with no need to impress, pretend, feel shame, or fear. Just relax in this place for the next minute or so. If your thoughts show up, acknowledge them and let them go. Just relax, let go, and enjoy the quiet.

When you're ready, open your eyes and continue.

Were you able to quiet your mind and be fully present in the moment? Was this a comfortable and familiar place? Could you hear the noise coming from your unhealthy habits of thinking over there in *that* chair?

In what ways would your life be different if YOU showed up here more frequently, fully present, fully engaged, listening more intently to the whispers, while solidly gripping the armrests of the Observer's Chair?

Once we recognize that we are not our unhealthy habits of thinking, we recognize these are just bad habits. In time, they lose their power over us. We—the Observer— finally inherit our rightful place, the Observer's Chair.

My Freedom Declaration

This day I will make the best day of my life. This day I will drink every minute to its full. I will savor its taste and give thanks. I will maketh every hour count and each minute I will trade only for something of value. — OG MANDINO

The flame that burns inside of me cries out—I have been uniquely shaped and molded and prepared for my life's mission. I matter!

I stand ready to be counted as a victor. No longer will I wallow in my misery. No longer will I focus on what is missing. I focus on what remains and what I can build with what I have.

Never again will I go down into that black hole seeking answers to that unanswerable question, "Why me?" I ask the rich and ennobling question, "Is anyone else suffering from a similar wound?"

Yes, it was painful. But I have willingly engraved these experiences on my heart so that I can have empathy for others.

I listen using my heart and it amplifies my intuition. I courageously ask empathetic questions that demonstrate my understanding. I take down walls of hate and suspicion and create connection.

There is finally purpose in my suffering—my experiences matter. Using these experiences, I choose to be and create a safe place for others. I choose to lift and build others. My soul is filled with joy overflowing and this joy is healing my soul.

When I am sitting in the Observer's Chair—being my true self—free from the noise of my unhealthy habits of thinking and the burdens of the past—I use my gift of vivid visualization to hear inspired whispers and see visions of possibilities. My passion is ignited.

I trust my intuition and act immediately on these whispers and visions, as if they were urgent assignments. I discover the validity of each and in so doing, I trust and am trusted. I know and am known. And this knowingness is the single greatest source for healing my self-esteem.

Epilogue:
TODAY I BEGIN A NEW LIFE

I hunger for success. I thirst for happiness and peace of mind. Lest I act I will perish in a life of failure, misery, and sleepless nights. I will command, and I will obey mine own command. I will act now.

— OG MANDINO

When was the last time someone cared enough about you to truly listen until you felt understood? I have asked that question thousands of times and received only a handful of examples. It is rare.

Where do these extraordinary and rare people get their wisdom? How do they know the right question to ask at just the right time? How is it that they make us feel safe and loved? How can they be so laser focused on another person?

Could it be that they have had similar experiences, but instead of going inside for answers, they have chosen to use these experiences to reach out and better understand others? Surely this is true.

As a coach, I have had the privilege of visiting this sacred space called wholeness and completeness—self-esteem—with thousands of extraordinary individuals. With grown men and women I have laughed and cried.

Like me, some had great parents; others did not. Some grew up in the lap of luxury, others in the depths of poverty. Some had been imprisoned by addictions; most were imprisoned by unhealthy habits of thinking. Some received extensive formal educations; others slugged it out at the University of Hard Knocks. Each had unique life experiences, yet all had one thing in common. When we began our journey together each person was dragging around a huge sack—a veritable treasure chest of experiences.

Learning the principles for healing self-esteem, they courageously emptied their sacks, let go of the pain and engraved each experience on their hearts. They have become better listeners, hearing things others miss. They ask empathetic questions based on *their* life experiences, questions others might fail to ask, questions that demonstrate understanding, questions that float effortlessly to the surface.

They are safe and create safe places where a person's wall of resistance can come down and connection at a deep and rich level can occur. They understand that healing in their souls comes only when they focus on serving others. They do not give from an empty cup, but one that is overflowing with joy. They continue to grow and stretch and become the people they were meant to become.

Life has provided experiences that have prepared each of them in unique ways. Each can say, "*I have chosen to be one of the rare ones, and there is value in rarity. Therefore, I am valuable.*" They discover that which had been a burden for so long can now be used as a blessing—for the benefit of others and ultimately for themselves.

These experiences have not only shaped our character, they have prepared us for what is coming. In the months and years to follow, the world will need people who have seen the dark night, who have stood on the proverbial ledge, and who have consciously chosen to turn back, sit in the Observer's Chair, and again experience the light of joy. These servant-leaders can listen differently and hear differently. They will know the questions to ask. They will be able to guide people away from the ledge.

I invite all who are riddled by pain or shame to hold their past experiences differently and to use them in the service of others—become the Observer! Become a masterful servant-leader.

In my book, *Today I Begin a New Life*, I share in great detail the principles, practices and processes for Connecting with People, Mental Creation and Physical Creation.

You will learn The Art of Connection as I share the practice of Intrinsic Validation. You will learn the five ways to use your gift of vivid visualization to manifest inspired ideas, impressions and solutions to problems that will ignite passion. You will learn how to stay present in the NOW in passion-driven action. Go online today at www.ogmandino.com for special offers including FREE coaching.

APPENDIX

Resources:

Here are the links for accessing the Intentional Creation Assessment and for accessing the Ten Scrolls, the Becoming Affirmations, and the Stillness Exercise.

Take the free Intentional Creation Assessment by logging on to: www.ogmandino.com/assessment

Access the audio mp3 files at: www.ogmandinogroup.com/audio

It's all FREE with only one stipulation—it is for your ears only and as a thank you for purchasing this book and taking on your life.

Understanding the Assessment

Here are some guidelines to assist you in identifying the intensity of an unhealthy habit of thinking. Refer to the results of your FREE Intentional Creation Assessment.

- If the color assigned to a Characteristic is blue, the underlying thoughts support you in sitting in the Observer's Chair.

- If a Characteristic is green, occasionally your unhealthy thoughts beckon you to sit in the wrong chair. This should be relatively easy to override.

- If the color is orange, the voice is becoming dominant and subsequently the temptation to move over is frequent and intense.

- If the color is red, the temptation is consistent and the voice clearly dominant.

Come in From the Storm Video Series

In 1987, as part of my healing, I wrote, produced, and directed a three-part series on the topic of child abuse prevention entitled, *Come in From the Storm.*

In Part I: *China Doll*, a young and emotionally abusive mother, played by Holly Anderson, finally surrenders and seeks assistance while her loving daughter, played by Tobi Bishop, gratefully listens through the door.

In Part II: *The Diary*, a young boy from the future, played by Emmanuel Lewis (Webster), travels back in time to visit with his father who is still a young boy, played by Bumper Robinson (*Night Court*). In a touching scene, Emmanuel's character pleads with his father to seek help and break the chains of abuse and change the future.

In Part III: *The Necklace*, a young girl, played by Tiffany Brissett (*Small Wonder*), talks with her father, played by Gordon Jump (*WKRP in Cincinnati* and the MayTag man) about a classmate and close friend who is suffering from interfamilial sexual abuse.

As it turned out, we were way ahead of our time. One school district back then reported after previewing the three films, "Thank goodness we don't have these kinds of problems in our schools." The statement would be comical if it weren't so tragic. Fortunately times are changing. We are becoming more aware.

Just a few weeks prior to the publication of this book, the Maryland School District licensed the digital rights to the series. Other states have purchased copies for every school. Over the last twenty-five years, thousands and thousands of copies have been distributed in the US, Canada, New Zealand and Australia.

The series still stands today as a testament to the very real damage caused by emotional, physical and sexual abuse and the need for intervention.

I have posted this three-part series on 'The Og Mandino YouTube Channel for all to view. The production is getting a little dated, but the content is not. May it serve.

Join us at:

www.ogmandino.com
www.ogmandinoblog.com
YouTube: Og Mandino Channel
Facebook: Og Mandino Author
Twitter: @TheOgGroup